true discipleship

a companion guide

true discipleship

a companion guide

THE

ART OF

FOLLOWING

JESUS

JOHN KOESSLER

MOODY PUBLISHERS
CHICAGO

© 2003 by
JOHN KOESSLER

Edited by Jim Vincent
Interior and Cover design: Ragont Design

Library of Congress Cataloging-in-Publication Data

Koessler, John, 1953-
 True discipleship: the art of following Jesus; A Companion Guide / John Koessler
    p. cm.
Includes bibliographical references.
 ISBN-13: 978-0-8024-1643-8
 1. Christian life. I. Title
 BV4501.3 .K64 2003
248.4—dc21

                                                                            2002151841
We hope you enjoy this book from Moody Publishers. Our goal is to provide high-quality, thought-provok-ing books and products that connect truth to your real needs and challenges. For more information on other books and products written and produced from a biblical perspective, go to www.moodypublishers.com or write to:

Moody Publishers
820 N. LaSalle Boulevard
Chicago, IL 60610

5 7 9 10 8 6

Printed in the United States of America

CONTENTS

THE
MARKS OF
DISCIPLESHIP

THE
MARK OF
GRACE

KEY PASSAGE: *By their fruit you will recognize them. Do people pick grapes from thornbushes, or figs from thistles? Likewise every good tree bears good fruit, but a bad tree bears bad fruit.*
(Matthew 7:16–17)

WISE WORDS

The soul has life communicated to it, so as through Christ's power to have inherent in itself a vital nature. In the soul where Christ savingly is, there he lives. He does not merely live without it, so as violently to actuate it, but he lives in it, so that the soul also is alive. Grace in the soul is as much from Christ as the light in a glass, held out in the sunbeams, is from the sun.
JONATHAN EDWARDS

God's free gift of justification, that is, pardon and acceptance here and now through Christ's perfect obedience culminating in his substitutionary sin bearing for us on the cross, is the basis on which the entire sanctifying process rests. . . . Holy people glory, not in their holiness, but in Christ's cross; for the holiest saint is never more than a justified sinner and never sees himself in any other way.
J. I. PACKER

THOUGHT STARTER

Has there ever been a time when you recognized that someone was a follower of Christ before they told you of their faith? What did you see in them that led you to conclude that they were a Christian? _____

_____

Can you think of a time when you were surprised to find that someone was a Christian? What was it about them that made you surprised to learn of their faith? _____

_____

Describe an occasion when someone recognized your commitment to Jesus Christ without your having to tell the person. _____

_____

SCRIPTURE STUDY

The life of discipleship is rooted in the grace of God. It begins in grace, is lived out in grace, and will be completed in grace. Discipleship is not so much a matter of doing the right things as it is one of cooperating with the grace of God. Everything we do as followers of Christ is a reflection of the life of Christ within us. Notice what the verses below have to say about the relationship between God's grace and the Christian life.

The Word became flesh and made his dwelling among us. We have seen his glory, the glory of the One and Only, who came from the Father, full of grace and truth. John testifies concerning him. He cries out, saying, "This was he of whom I said, 'He who comes after me has surpassed me because he was before me.'" From the fullness of his grace we have all received one blessing after another. For the law was given through Moses; grace and truth came through Jesus Christ. (John 1:14–17)

For it is by grace you have been saved, through faith—and this not from yourselves, it is the gift of God—not by works, so that no one can boast. (Ephesians 2:8–9)

What do these verses teach about the origin of grace? It is a gift from God

What do they say about the relationship between grace and faith?

Grace is the foundation of the Christian life. There is no salvation apart from grace. Why is grace so important?

How does God's grace affect those who receive it?

What do the following verses, all from the book of Acts, teach about the source, recipients, and effects of God's grace?

	Source of Grace	Recipients	Effects of Grace
Acts 4:31–37	the Lord	The multitude	no lack, healing of the sick
Acts 6:8	Faith + power from God	For the people	Performed great things
Acts 11:19–23	From God	Many people besides the Jews	many believed and turned to the Lord
Acts 14:3	the Lord	Jews + Greeks	Bearing witness + performing signs + wonders

	Source of Grace	Recipients	Effects of Grace
Acts 14:26	God	Those who spread the word	Commended
Acts 15:11	By God	Gentiles	Salvation
Acts 15:40			
Acts 18:27			
Acts 20:24			
Acts 20:32			

In Matthew 7:16–17, Jesus says that it is possible to recognize a false prophet by the spiritual fruit that is produced in his or her life. In what way is this also true of a disciple? _____

_____

_____

MY RESPONSE

1. Describe the time when you recognized your need for God's grace and the forgiveness of Christ. _____

_____

_____

2. Think of someone who has not heard your story. Pray that God will give you an opportunity to share it with him or her in the next week. _____

_____

_____

CONCLUSION

Discipleship is not primarily a matter of what we do. It is an outgrowth of who and what we are in Christ. Yet if this is true, it is reasonable for others to expect to see proof of the reality of our commitment to Christ reflected in the way that we live. Jesus' observation regarding false prophets is also true of disciples. They are recognizable by the fruit they produce: "By their fruit you will recognize them. Do people pick grapes from thornbushes, or figs from thistles? Likewise every good tree bears good fruit, but a bad tree bears bad fruit" (Matthew 7:16–17). So what are the marks of a disciple? Jesus Himself identified several important characteristics; we'll look at them in upcoming lessons.

PRAYER

Write a prayer of response. If you have not trusted in Jesus Christ as your Savior and Lord, ask Him to forgive you of your sin and to take control of your life. If you have already done so, thank God for His grace and ask Him to use this workbook to strengthen your spiritual life.

THE MARK OF BAPTISM

KEY PASSAGE: *Then Jesus came to them and said, "All authority in heaven and on earth has been given to me. Therefore go and make disciples of all nations, baptizing them in the name of the Father and of the Son and of the Holy Spirit, and teaching them to obey everything I have commanded you."* (Matthew 28:18–20)

WISE WORDS

But baptism serves as our confession before men. Indeed, it is the mark by which we publicly profess that we wish to be reckoned God's people; by which we testify that we agree in worshipping the same God, in one religion with all Christians; by which finally we openly affirm our faith.

JOHN CALVIN

Experiencing baptism doesn't make you right with God. The water of baptism does not wash away the guilt of your disobedience to the laws of God. Rather it is the grace of God, through the work of Jesus Christ that brings you into God's family and favor. That doesn't mean, however, that baptism is unimportant. Although baptism is never equated with faith or salvation in the New Testament, it is closely associated with both.

DONALD WHITNEY

THOUGHT STARTER

Have you been baptized? Why or why not? _____

_____

_____

What would you say to someone who said that they had trusted in Christ for salvation but did not want to be baptized? _____

_____

_____

SCRIPTURE STUDY

The first mark of a disciple is baptism. It is one of the first acts that identifies us as followers of Jesus Christ and initiates us into a life of obedience. When Jesus commissioned the church to go and make disciples of all nations, He identified baptism as the first of the two central tasks of disciple making in Matthew 28:19.

Read Matthew 28:18–20 and then answer the following questions.

With what does Jesus associate baptism in Matthew 28:18–20? _____

_____

_____

Who is to be baptized? _____

_____

_____

What is the significance of baptizing "in the name" of the Father, Son, and Holy Spirit? _____

_____

_____

What shall we say, then? Shall we go on sinning so that grace may increase? By no means! We died to sin; how can we live in it any longer? Or don't you know that all of us who were baptized into Christ Jesus were baptized into his death? We were therefore buried with him through baptism into death in order that, just as Christ was raised from the dead through the glory of the Father, we too may live a new life. (Romans 6:1–4)

Baptism is a rite with both individual and corporate significance. What do these verses tell us about what baptism symbolizes for the individual? _____

_____

_____

Water baptism signifies the believer's spiritual union with Christ. How does this help you to understand Paul's meaning when he says that believers have been "baptized" into Christ's death? _____

_____

_____

According to Paul, what practical implications does this have for daily living? _____

_____

_____

Where does Paul say the power to live this new life comes from? _____

_____

_____

For we were all baptized by one Spirit into one body—whether Jews or Greeks, slave or free—and we were all given the one Spirit to drink. (1 Corinthians 12:13)

Water baptism also indicates that the believer has been joined to the larger fellowship of the church. What does Paul say that believers have in common with everyone else who has trusted in Christ, according to 1 Corinthians 12:13? _____

_____

_____

What implications does this have for the way you view other believers? _____

_____

_____

Those who are joined to Christ by faith are also joined to other believers in the fellowship of the Spirit, Paul tells the Corinthians—and us. They confess the same Lord and are indwelt by the same Spirit. In a sense, baptism is as much a symbol of commitment to the church as it is a pledge of fidelity to Christ.

> *[Christ] was put to death in the body but made alive by the Spirit, through whom also he went and preached to the spirits in prison who disobeyed long ago when God waited patiently in the days of Noah while the ark was being built. In it only a few people, eight in all, were saved through water, and this water symbolizes baptism that now saves you also—not the removal of dirt from the body but the pledge of a good conscience toward God. It saves you by the resurrection of Jesus Christ, who has gone into heaven and is at God's right hand—with angels, authorities and powers in submission to him. (1 Peter 3:18–22)*

To what Old Testament event does Peter compare the waters of baptism? _____

_____

_____

What do you think Peter means when he says that the waters of Noah "symbolize" baptism? What do the two events seem to have in common? _____

_____

_____

The text does not say that Noah was saved "from" water but "through" it. Noah and his family passed through the waters of judgment but were spared its effects because Noah had believed God and had entered the safety of the ark. In a similar way, believers passed through divine judgment when it was poured out on Christ. They have been spared its effects because they have believed the gospel and are safe "in Christ."

In what sense does Peter say baptism "saves"? Is it the ritual itself? _____

_____

_____

The Bible does not teach that the rite of baptism in and of itself conveys the forgiveness of sin. Although Peter says that baptism "now saves you," he clarifies that it is actually the work of Christ that does the saving and not the water of baptism (1 Peter 3:21).

Peter uses the language of contractual agreements to describe baptism. The Greek term that is translated "pledge" literally meant "answer" and referred to a legal procedure in which questions were asked and commitments made on the part of those who entered into a contractual arrangement with one another. Baptism is a pledge of commitment made to God that springs from the cleansing that has come through faith in Christ.

In what sense might it also be said that God is making a pledge in baptism? _____
_____
_____

With what is baptism linked in the following verses?

Acts 2:38; 22:16 _____
_____
_____

Romans 6:4; Colossians 2:11–12 _____
_____
_____

What changes can you point to as evidence of the new life God has promised to those who are in Christ? _____
_____
_____

Read Galatians 5:17–24 and Ephesians 2:1–10. In the boxes below write what these passages say was true of us while we were in the sinful nature and what is true of us now that we are in Christ.

Old Self	New Self

MY RESPONSE

The ordinance of baptism has been compared to one's wedding vows. Write out a "pledge" of commitment to Christ that reflects the spiritual truths symbolized in baptism.

_____

_____

_____

_____

CONCLUSION

Because it symbolizes the believer's union with Christ through the Holy Spirit, baptism also contains an implicit promise of transformation. Baptism's picture of burial and resurrection points to a radical change in the believer's nature. Those who are in Christ are alive in a way that was not true prior to Christ. Paul links baptism with the Old Testament rite of circumcision and says that those who have been baptized have "put off" the old nature (Colossians 2:11–12). All who enter into a relationship with Christ die to the old self. Positively, they have been "clothed" with Christ (Galatians 3:27). God's promise in baptism is the promise of forgiveness and a new life. My commitment in baptism is the pledge to live in accordance with the change that Christ has brought about in me by His death and resurrection.

PRAYER

Use what you have written above as the basis for a prayer of commitment to Christ.

THE
MARK OF
OBEDIENCE

KEY PASSAGE: *To the Jews who had believed him, Jesus said, "If you hold to my teaching, you are really my disciples. Then you will know the truth, and the truth will set you free."* (John 8:31–32)

WISE WORDS

A little thing is a little thing, but faithfulness in little things is a very great thing.
AMY CARMICHAEL

Our Lord never enforces obedience; He does not take means to make me do what He wants. At certain times I wish God would master me and make me do the thing, but He will not; in other moods I wish He would leave me alone, but He does not.
A. W. TOZER

THOUGHT STARTER

Think of a time when, even though you found it difficult, you chose to obey Christ. What made the decision to obey so difficult? _____

_____

_____

Why did you choose to obey rather than disobey? _____

_____

_____

The Bible tells us that we are saved by grace and not by our own effort (Ephesians 2:8). Why should we be concerned about obedience since it is not the cause of our salvation? _____

_____

_____

SCRIPTURE STUDY

True discipleship is marked by obedience. The second major component of Jesus' directive in the Great Commission was to teach disciples "to obey everything I have commanded you" (Matthew 28:20). Obedience is not optional for the Christian. As Jesus' popularity increased, He warned followers that obedience would be the true test of their discipleship. According to John 8:31–32, "To the Jews who had believed him,

Jesus said, 'If you hold to my teaching, you are really my disciples. Then you will know the truth, and the truth will set you free.'" Passages like this can make us uncomfortable because they seem to imply that our status as disciples is earned. There is a condition here, but its force is one of evidence rather than of cause. Jesus did not say that we become disciples by holding to His teaching.

Read John 8:31–32 again. Which comes first in these verses, discipleship or obedience? _____

_____

_____

What difference does this make? _____

_____

_____

Commenting on the passage, New Testament scholar Leon Morris explained, "Jesus' words then are meant to drive home to formal and casual adherents something of the meaning of true discipleship. If men in any sense believe in Him it is important that they be led to see what real faith means."[1] The obedience spoken of by Jesus is proof that those who obey are truly Christ's disciples in the first place. This may sound like a semantic game, but the order is vitally important. If discipleship depends upon my obedience, then the primary focus of Jesus' statement is on my ability to comply with all that God commands. If, on the other hand, obedience depends upon the reality of my discipleship relationship with Jesus Christ, the primary focus is on Christ Himself.

The Scriptures speak of two very different kinds of obedience: one is legalistic; the other is rooted in grace. Legalistic obedience follows God's commands in order to earn a righteous standing in God's sight. Grace-rooted obedience recognizes that righteousness can only be received as a gift. It cannot be earned as a wage. My obedience is an expression of gratitude for that gift.

After each of the following Scripture passages, indicate the type of obedience being described and briefly explain why you think it falls into that category.

Knowing that a man is not justified by the works of the Law, but through faith in Christ Jesus, even we have believed in Christ Jesus, that we might be justified by faith in Christ, and not by the works of the Law; since by the works of the Law shall no flesh be justified. (Galatians 2:16 NASB)

Is Galatians 2:16 describing legalistic or grace-based obedience? Why? _____

_____

_____

I would like to learn just one thing from you: Did you receive the Spirit by observing the law, or by believing what you heard? Are you so foolish? After beginning with the Spirit, are you now trying to attain your goal by human effort? (Galatians 3:2–3)

Is Galatians 3:2–3 describing legalistic or grace-based obedience? Why? _____

_____

_____

Consider Abraham: "He believed God, and it was credited to him as righteousness." Understand, then, that those who believe are children of Abraham. The Scripture foresaw that God would justify the Gentiles by faith, and announced the gospel in advance to Abraham: "All nations will be blessed through you." So those who have faith are blessed along with Abraham, the man of faith. (Galatians 3:6–9)

Is Galatians 3:6–9 describing legalistic or grace-based obedience? Why? _____

_____

_____

Again I declare to every man who lets himself be circumcised that he is obligated to obey the whole law. You who are trying to be justified by law have been alienated from Christ; you have fallen away from grace. (Galatians 5:3–4)

Is Galatians 5:3–4 describing legalistic or grace-based obedience? Why? _____

_____

_____

How does legalistic obedience differ from grace-rooted obedience? _____

_____

_____

Legalistic obedience is the polar opposite of grace-rooted obedience. Although the objective in legalistic obedience may seem like a good one—the observance of God's commands—it is flawed because it overestimates the human capacity to comply. It produces an obedience that is grounded in self rather than in God.

What do the following passages indicate is the difference with grace-based obedience?

John 14:15 _____

_____

_____

John 14:24 _____

_____

_____

Romans 1:5 _____

_____

_____

Grace, like legalism, also has obedience to God's commands as its objective. According to Romans 2:14, it is not those who hear God's Law who are declared righteous but those who obey it. The chief difference with grace-rooted obedience is that it is grounded in Christ's righteousness rather than my own. It is "the obedience that comes from faith" (Romans 1:5). Legalism, on the other hand, produces an obedience that is grounded in self rather than in God.

What shall we say, then? Is the law sin? Certainly not! Indeed I would not have known what sin was except through the law. For I would not have known what coveting really was if the law had not said, "Do not covet." But sin, seizing the opportunity afforded by the commandment, produced in me every kind of covetous desire. For apart from law, sin is dead. Once I was alive apart from law; but when the commandment came, sin sprang to life and I died. I found that the very commandment that was intended to bring life actually brought death. For sin, seizing the opportunity afforded by the commandment, deceived me, and through the commandment put me to death. So then, the law is holy, and the commandment is holy, righteous and good. Did that which is good, then, become death to me? By no means! But in order that sin might be recognized as sin, it produced death in me through what was good, so that through the commandment sin might become utterly sinful. We know that the law is spiritual; but I am unspiritual, sold as a slave to sin. (Romans 7:7–14)

If God's Law is "holy, righteous and good," why can't we depend upon it to make us righteous before God? ___

_____

_____

What does Paul say was God's purpose in giving the Law? _____

_____

_____

What does the Law teach us about the nature of sin? _____

_____

_____

What does the Law teach us about ourselves? _____

_____

_____

What does it teach us about Christ? _____

_____

_____

MY RESPONSE

1. Identify an example of grace-rooted obedience from the past week. _____

_____

_____

2. In what way did it require the grace of God? _____

_____

_____

3. Identify a specific area where you know you will need to obey God in the near future. _____

_____

_____

4. What kind of grace is needed in order for you to comply? _____

_____

_____

5. What plans have you made to obey? _____

_____

_____

CONCLUSION

For the Christian, faith *is* obedience, because it focuses on the one who obeyed all God's commands on my behalf. When I trusted in Jesus Christ, my faith was credited to me as righteousness (Romans 4:5). Grace-rooted obedience recognizes that righteousness can only be received as a gift. It cannot be earned as a wage. My present obedience is an expression of gratitude for that gift. It is not surprising, then, that Jesus repeatedly identified love as the primary motive for obedience. "If you love me," He told His disciples, "you will obey what I command" (John 14:15). "He who does not love me," He warned, "will not obey my teaching" (John 14:24).

PRAYER

Write a brief prayer asking for God's help to follow through on the area of obedience described above.

_____

_____

_____

_____

_____

_____

THE
MARK OF
SPIRITUAL FRUIT

KEY PASSAGE: *If you remain in me and my words remain in you, ask whatever you wish, and it will be given you. This is to my Father's glory, that you bear much fruit, showing yourselves to be my disciples.* (John 15:7–8)

WISE WORDS

Every plant must have both soil and root. Without both of these there can be no life, no growth, no fruit.
HORATIUS BONAR

Samuel Coleridge, the British poet and philosopher, was arguing with a man who believed that religious instruction was harmful to children. The man believed that children should not be burdened with their parents' notions about God. He reasoned that this would make them better equipped to make their own decisions about faith when they reached the age of discretion. Coleridge strongly disagreed but did not argue with the man. Instead, he invited him to step into his garden. It had been neglected for some time and was overgrown with weeds. "Do you call this a garden!" the man declared. "There are nothing but weeds here!" Coleridge smiled slyly upon hearing the man's criticism. "Well, you see," Coleridge explained, "I did not wish to infringe upon the liberty of the garden in any way. I was just giving the garden a chance to express itself and to choose its own production."

THOUGHT STARTER

How is the believer's spiritual life like a garden? _____

_____

_____

What kind of "soil" is necessary before we can produce spiritual fruit? _____

_____

_____

Should you be concerned if you do not see in your life any evidence of spiritual fruit? Why or why not?

_____

_____

_____

SCRIPTURE STUDY

According to Jesus, those who abide in Christ produce spiritual fruit (John 15:5). Results are expected of the disciple, but they are the results of being connected to the vine. It is the life of the vine that generates the fruit. Yet there is clearly an element of personal responsibility involved in the fruit-bearing process: The believer has the responsibility of abiding. Still, it is not possible to produce fruit apart from Christ. When I abide, I am conscious that everything that Christ commands of me Christ must also produce in me. It is a state that might be described as "actively passive." It is both active and passive at the same time.

Read John 15:1–17 and in the table below summarize what is said about the Father, Jesus Christ, and the believer in these verses.

Verse	The Father	Jesus Christ	The Believer
v. 1	The Father is the gardener.	Jesus is the vine.	
v. 2	The Father does the pruning.		Branches that bear fruit are pruned.
v. 3			
v. 4			
v. 5			
v. 6			
v. 7			
v. 8			
v. 9			
v. 10			
v. 11			
v. 12			
v. 13			
v. 14			
v. 15			
v. 16			
v. 17			

What does Jesus say is the secret to a life of spiritual fruitfulness in these verses? _____

_____

_____

How would you describe the relationship between the branch and the vine in Jesus' metaphor? _____

_____

_____

What is being stressed here, the action of bearing fruit or the life-giving nature of the vine? What is the relationship between these two? _____

_____

_____

How do the Bible and prayer play a part in the fruit bearing process, according to Jesus? _____

_____

_____

What is Jesus saying about the life of discipleship besides, "Read the Scriptures and pray"? _____

_____

_____

MY RESPONSE

1. In what ways are you currently "abiding" in Christ? _____

_____

_____

2. What evidence is there that you are bearing "much fruit" for Christ? _____

_____

_____

3. Identify at least one area where you would like Christ to produce even more fruit. _____

_____

_____

CONCLUSION

According to Jesus, the branch draws its life from its connection to the vine. If it were to be severed from the vine, it would wither and die. The same is true of the believer. We have no spiritual life apart from Christ. He is the source of our life and the ultimate cause of fruitfulness. The Christian life is simply the life of Christ reflected in our own lives. It has both passive and active dimensions. It is passive in that Christ alone is its source. I cannot give life to myself. No human effort can add to what Christ has already done. Yet there is also an active dimension to the spiritual life. We make choices and take actions that enable us to access the life of Christ and bring it to bear on daily living. We read the Bible and pray. We worship God and serve one another. In the natural realm, the farmer plants the seed and cultivates the crop but cannot make the plant grow. This is also true in the spiritual realm. Human effort is involved but the growth comes from God. As Paul puts it, "I planted the seed, Apollos watered it, but God made it grow" (1 Corinthians 3:6).

PRAYER

Write a prayer asking God to produce spiritual fruit in the area identified above. Be specific in what you request.

_____

_____

_____

_____

_____

THE
MARK OF
LOVE

KEY PASSAGE: *"A new command I give you: Love one another. As I have loved you, so you must love one another. By this all men will know that you are my disciples, if you love one another."* (John 13:34–35)

WISE WORDS

Love is the abridgement of all theology.
                    FRANCIS DESALES

The worldly man treats certain people kindly because he "likes" them: the Christian, trying to treat everyone kindly, finds himself liking more and more people as he goes on—including people he could not even have imagined himself liking at the beginning.
                    C. S. LEWIS

THOUGHT STARTER

Who are we commanded to love? _____

_____

_____

Do we have a special obligation to love some more than others? Why or why not? _____

_____

_____

Think of someone who has shown love to you recently. How did he or she show it? _____

_____

_____

SCRIPTURE STUDY

On one occasion an expert in the law stood up to test Jesus. "Teacher," he asked, "what must I do to inherit eternal life?" "What is written in the Law?" he replied. "How do you read it?" He answered: "'Love the Lord your God with all your heart and with all your soul and with all your strength and with all your mind'; and, 'Love your neighbor as yourself.'" "You have answered correctly," Jesus replied. "Do this and you will live." But he wanted to justify himself, so he asked Jesus, "And who is my neighbor?" (Luke 10:25–29)

Who, according to Jesus, has first claim on our love? _____

_____

_____

Who are we to love in addition? _____

_____

_____

Why is the order of these commands important? _____

_____

_____

What question did this religious expert ask after Jesus told him that he had answered the question correctly?

_____

_____

_____

What motivated his second question? _____

_____

_____

Jesus answered his question by telling a story about a man traveling from Jerusalem to Jericho. Read it in Luke 10:29–37. Then answer the following questions.

Why do you suppose the priest and Levite passed by without helping the man? _____

_____

_____

What "good" reasons might they have had for their actions? (cf. Leviticus 21:10–11; Numbers 5:2; 19:13)?

_____

_____

_____

What "good" reasons might the Samaritan have had for passing by (cf. John 4:9, 20)? _____

_____

_____

In what sense was the Samaritan a neighbor? _____

_____

_____

What does this parable tell you about the kind of love Christ expects from those who are His disciples?

_____

_____

_____

We love him because he first loved us. (1 John 4:19 KJV)

Lovers often adopt the same interests; it's one of the characteristics of love. People who have been married for a long time often begin to talk like one another. Some even begin to resemble each other physically. The same principle holds true in our relationship with God. If we love God, we will want to be like Him. We will love what God loves. This would be easy if those whom God loves were always lovable. Fortunately, He has a penchant for loving the unlovely and for setting His affection on those who don't love Him back. We shouldn't be surprised. This was our own experience. We love Him because He first loved us.

In what ways does love differ from a "mood"? _____

_____

_____

What implications does this have as far as your response to Christ's command is concerned? _____

_____

_____

How does this help you to obey Christ's command to love others? _____

_____

_____

What does John say about the relationship between love and action in 1 John 3:17–20? _____

_____

_____

MY RESPONSE

1. Rewrite Jesus' command in John 13:34–35. In the place of the phrase "one another" write the name of someone Christ is calling you to show love to today. _____

_____

_____

2. Think of at least one practical way that you can show love to the person you have identified on page 26.

_____

_____

_____

CONCLUSION

Our obligation to love as Christ loves is challenged by today's confused notions about the nature of love. True, biblical love is active. It is reflected more in what we do than in how we feel. Today's society views love primarily as an emotion. Although emotion plays a part, its role is secondary. Moods change from day to day. I can feel affectionate toward someone today and cold toward the same person tomorrow. Love involves an exercise of the will. Biblical love isn't necessarily feeling good about another person. It is acting towards them in a way that is pleasing to God and appropriate to their need.

PRAYER

Pray for the person you have identified above. Pray for yourself that God will make you a channel of love to that person.

NOTE

1. Leon Morris, *The Gospel According to John* (Grand Rapids: Eerdmans, 1971), 455.

THE
COST OF
DISCIPLESHIP

TAKING
UP THE
CROSS

KEY PASSAGE: *Then he said to them all: "If anyone would come after me, he must deny himself and take up his cross daily and follow me.*
(Luke 9:23)

WISE WORDS

Although we owe God gratitude, although we owe much to His love, we owe nothing to His justice; for Christ in that hour took all our sins, past, present, and future. He was punished for them all there and then, that we might never be punished, because He suffered in our stead.
CHARLES SPURGEON

Must Jesus bear the cross alone, and all the world go free?
No, there's a cross for everyone, and there's a cross for me.
THOMAS SHEPHERD

THOUGHT STARTER

What do you think of when you see a cross? _____

_____

_____

What do most people mean when they say that they speak of something as their "cross to bear"? _____

_____

_____

If Jesus' death on the cross paid for your sins, why does He ask you to take up the cross and follow Him?

_____

_____

_____

SCRIPTURE STUDY

In Jesus' day, the cross was an instrument of death—one of the cruelest forms of punishment in the ancient world. Yet Jesus' death on the cross paid for mankind's sins and brought all who would believe back to God and the hope of eternal life. Jesus has called His disciples to take up their cross daily and follow Him.

Anyone who loves his father or mother more than me is not worthy of me; anyone who loves his son or daughter more than me is not worthy of me; and anyone who does not take his cross and follow me is not worthy of me. (Matthew 10:37–38)

On what occasion, according to Matthew 10:5, did Jesus issue this command? _____

_____

_____

What did He say would happen to His followers because of their testimony for Him, according to Matthew 10:17–23? _____

_____

_____

What did He mean when He said, "A student is not above his teacher, nor a servant above his master" (Matthew 10:24)? _____

_____

_____

Read Luke 14:25–33. Then answer the following questions.

This passage recounts another occasion when Jesus called those who followed Him to take up the cross. Although the language is similar to Matthew 10:37–38, there are some differences worth noting. In Matthew 10:38 the call to take up the cross is given to the Twelve. Who is Jesus addressing in Luke 14:26–27? _____

_____

_____

How should our commitment to Christ compare with our commitment to others who are important to us?

_____

_____

_____

This does not mean that I regard my parents, brothers and sisters, or spouse as unimportant. I continue to have an obligation to love and respect them. The "hatred" spoken of in this passage is by way of comparison. It is hyperbolic language meant to drive home my obligation to love Christ more than any other and to defer to Him in all my decisions. The command to take up the cross involves a personal commitment to Jesus Christ that takes precedence over everything else. It calls me to cherish Christ more than any other human bond.

How should we approach discipleship, according to Luke 14:28–33? _____

_____

_____

Jesus gives two examples of "counting the cost." What are they? _____

_____

_____

In view of these examples, what conclusion does Jesus expect those who count the cost of discipleship to reach?

_____

_____

_____

What danger does Christ want the crowd to avoid? _____

_____

_____

Jesus compared the disciple to a man who builds a tower or a king who plans to go to war with another king. Both would estimate the potential cost of such a project before embarking on it. Those who answer the call to discipleship must do so thoughtfully. Christ is not looking for rash decisions that are made in the heat of the moment and then easily abandoned. Those who answer the call must know what Christ requires—He asks for everything.

The implication is clear. Those who count the cost will realize that they do not have the resources in themselves to be faithful. Christ demands far more than our best effort. He is not satisfied with anything less than "everything." His own death and resurrection, however, mean that what Christ requires of those who would be His disciples, He also supplies.

From that time on Jesus began to explain to his disciples that he must go to Jerusalem and suffer many things at the hands of the elders, chief priests and teachers of the law, and that he must be killed and on the third day be raised to life. Peter took him aside and began to rebuke him. "Never, Lord!" he said. "This shall never happen to you!" Jesus turned and said to Peter, "Get behind me, Satan! You are a stumbling block to me; you do not have in mind the things of God, but the things of men." Then Jesus said to his disciples, "If anyone would come after me, he must deny himself and take up his cross and follow me. For whoever wants to save his life will lose it, but whoever loses his life for me will find it. What good will it be for a man if he gains the whole world, yet forfeits his soul? Or what can a man give in exchange for his soul? (Matthew 16:21–26)

This is the third time Jesus called His disciples to carry the cross. What precipitated the command? _____

_____

_____

Why do you think Jesus felt it was necessary to repeat this command to His disciples? _____

_____

_____

Are any of the things that Jesus mentions in this passage matters over which you have no control? _____

_____

_____

What does it mean to "take up the cross"? _____

_____

_____

MY RESPONSE

1. In what areas of your life is Christ calling you to take up the cross? _____

_____

_____

2. For each of the areas listed below, describe the challenges that have come about as a result of your commitment to Christ and what it means to "take up the cross" in each situation.

Family. *The challenges I face are:* _____

In this case, taking up the cross will mean: _____

_____

_____

Friends. *The challenges I face are:* _____

In this case, taking up the cross will mean: _____

_____

_____

School. *The challenges I face are:* _____

In this case, taking up the cross will mean: _____

_____

_____

Work. *The challenges I face are:* _____

In this case, taking up the cross will mean: _____

_____

_____

Unbelievers. *The challenges I face are:* _____

In this case, taking up the cross will mean: _____

_____

_____

Other believers. *The challenges I face are:*_____

In this case, taking up the cross will mean: _____

_____

_____

CONCLUSION

"Must Jesus bear the cross alone, and all the world go free?" asks the old hymn. "No," the hymn writer replies, "there's a cross for everyone, and there's a cross for me." We don't hear these words sung much in the church today. Perhaps that is because we think its message is not upbeat enough for modern audiences. Yet Jesus makes it clear that every disciple must bear the cross. In the Roman world the cross was an instrument of torture and execution. It was a symbol of shame (Hebrews 12:2). When Jesus called upon those who would follow Him to take up their own cross, He gave notice that the disciple's lot would be one of self-denial and death to the old nature. Most of the apostles eventually suffered martyrdom as a result of their commitment to Christ, but the kind of cross bearing that is commanded of all disciples is more enduring. It is not a single event but something that Christ calls us to practice every day.

PRAYER

Choose an area from the list above. Pray a prayer of commitment and ask Christ to help you in that area.

THE
LIVING
DEAD

KEY PASSAGE: *As for you, you were dead in your transgressions and sins, in which you used to live when you followed the ways of this world and of the ruler of the kingdom of the air, the spirit who is now at work in those who are disobedient. All of us also lived among them at one time, gratifying the cravings of our sinful nature and following its desires and thoughts. Like the rest, we were by nature objects of wrath.* (Ephesians 2:1–3)

WISE WORDS

By and large, dying is a messy business.
                    SHERWIN B. NULAND

What a wretched man I am! Who will rescue me from this body of death?
                    ROMANS 7:24

THOUGHT STARTER

What was your life like before trusting in Christ? _____

_____

_____

What is it like now that you have trusted in Christ? _____

_____

_____

What has been the greatest change that you have experienced? _____

_____

_____

SCRIPTURE STUDY

As for you, you were dead in your transgressions and sins, in which you used to live when you followed the ways of this world and of the ruler of the kingdom of the air, the spirit who is now at work in those who are disobedient. All of us also lived among them at one time, gratifying the cravings of our sinful nature and following its desires and thoughts. Like the rest, we were by nature objects of wrath. (Ephesians 2:1–3)

Prior to faith in Christ we were spiritually dead. What was this condition like, according to Ephesians 2:1–3? _____

_____

_____

Are the spiritually dead also spiritually inactive? _____

_____

_____

What "spirit" do those who are spiritually dead follow? _____

_____

_____

How does spiritual death affect one's desires, thoughts, and goals? _____

_____

_____

How does it affect one's relationship to God? _____

_____

_____

In what sense might it be said that those who are dead spiritually are the "living dead"? _____

_____

_____

Read Galatians 5:17–21. Identify some of the "acceptable" forms the practices and attitudes included in this list take today.

Which of these "acts of the sinful nature" are most likely to show up in your life? _____

_____

_____

Where do they usually appear? _____

_____

_____

What form do they take? _____

_____

_____

But because of his great love for us, God, who is rich in mercy, made us alive with Christ even when we were dead in transgressions—it is by grace you have been saved. And God raised us up with Christ and seated us with him in the heavenly realms in Christ Jesus, in order that in the coming ages he might show the incomparable riches of his grace, expressed in his kindness to us in Christ Jesus. For it is by grace you have been saved, through faith—and this not from yourselves, it is the gift of God—not by works, so that no one can boast. For we are God's workmanship, created in Christ Jesus to do good works, which God prepared in advance for us to do. (Ephesians 2:4–10)

What does Paul say is the current state of those who are in Christ? _____

_____

_____

In what sense are we "seated" with Christ? _____

_____

_____

How should we respond to God's grace, according to verse 10? _____

_____

_____

Pride, selfish ambition, and jealousy are as much expressions of the sinful nature as drunkenness and sexual immorality. Even religious zeal, when it is not rooted in the grace of God that comes through Jesus Christ, is an expression of the flesh (Philippians 3:3–9). If this is the constant state of all those who are outside Christ, it is also clear that it is the former state of all those who are now a part of Christ. We who were once dead in trespasses and sins have been "made alive" in Christ (Ephesians 2:5).

MY RESPONSE

1. Contrast the experience of physical death with the experience of physical life.

Death	**Life**
_____	_____
_____	_____
_____	_____

2. How has this contrast been reflected in your spiritual experience? _____

_____

_____

3. Where in your life do you see evidence of the kind of "good works" mentioned in Ephesians 2:10? _____

_____

_____

CONCLUSION

Those who are in the flesh are the "living dead." They live (or more literally "walk") in their transgressions and sins. This means that they are in a state of rebellion against God, and everything they do can only serve to gratify the cravings of the sinful nature in thought and deed. They have no other capacity. This may sound as though their lives were marked by a continual orgy, but the flesh also has many "respectable" avenues in which to manifest itself. Pride, selfish ambition, and jealousy are as much expressions of the sinful nature as drunkenness and sexual immorality (Galatians 5:17–21). Even religious zeal, when it is not rooted in the grace of God that comes through Jesus Christ, is an expression of the flesh (Philippians 3:3–9).

PRAYER

Read Ephesians 2:1–10 again and thank God for each of the changes mentioned in these verses.

THE CROSS
AND THE
FLESH

KEY PASSAGE: *What shall we say, then? Shall we go on sinning so that grace may increase? By no means! We died to sin; how can we live in it any longer?*
(Romans 6:1–2)

WISE WORDS

If sensuality were happiness, beasts were happier than men; but human felicity is lodged in the soul, not in the flesh.

SENECA

Many a solo is sung to show off; many a sermon is preached as an exhibition of talent; many a church is founded as a slap to some other church. Even missionary activity may become competitive, and soul-winning may degenerate into a sort of brush-salesman project to satisfy the flesh.

A. W. TOZER

THOUGHT STARTER

What is the difference between "flesh" used in a purely physical sense (i.e., the skin that covers your bones) and "flesh" in the spiritual sense? _____

_____

_____

Are Christians in "the flesh"? Explain your answer. _____

_____

_____

SCRIPTURE STUDY

The work of Christ has changed the believer's relationship to God. Those who are in Christ have been forgiven and are God's children. It has also changed the believer's relationship to self. The area of greatest change in this respect has to do with what the Bible refers to as "the flesh."

But because of his great love for us, God, who is rich in mercy, made us alive with Christ even when we were dead in transgressions—it is by grace you have been saved. (Ephesians 2:4–5)

If being dead in trespasses and sins is the condition of those living in the flesh, what is the condition of those who are living in Christ? _____

_____

_____

What was our condition before we were made alive? What is it now? _____

_____

_____

How did the cross of Christ play a role in this change? _____

_____

_____

What shall we say, then? Shall we go on sinning so that grace may increase? By no means! We died to sin; how can we live in it any longer? . . . In the same way, count yourselves dead to sin but alive to God in Christ Jesus. Therefore do not let sin reign in your mortal body so that you obey its evil desires. Do not offer the parts of your body to sin, as instruments of wickedness, but rather offer yourselves to God, as those who have been brought from death to life; and offer the parts of your body to him as instruments of righteousness. (Romans 6:1–2, 11–13)

What do you think Paul means when he tells his readers to "count themselves dead"? _____

_____

_____

How does he describe the condition of someone who allows the flesh to control their thoughts and actions?

_____

_____

_____

Paul urges his readers to "offer" themselves to God and to "offer" their bodies as instruments of righteousness. What kind of language is this? _____

_____

_____

It is significant that Paul uses the language of worship when he urges his readers not to live in the flesh. When he tells his readers to "offer" themselves, this is the language of sacrifice. It is also the language of service. Believers are priests and servants. When we offer our lives in obedience, it is both an act of worship and the reasonable service of those who have been purchased by Christ (cf. Romans 12:1–2).

Read Romans 7:14–22. Then answer the following questions.

Does the work of the Cross eliminate the presence of the sinful nature? _____

_____

_____

How does Paul describe his struggle with the flesh in these verses? _____

_____

_____

The mind of sinful man is death, but the mind controlled by the Spirit is life and peace; the sinful mind is hostile to God. It does not submit to God's law, nor can it do so. Those controlled by the sinful nature cannot please God. (Romans 8:6–8)

Why are those who allow themselves to be controlled by the sinful nature unable to please God? _____

_____

_____

What role does the mind play in this? _____

_____

_____

In view of this, what does it mean to "reckon" yourself to be dead to sin? _____

_____

_____

You, however, are controlled not by the sinful nature but by the Spirit, if the Spirit of God lives in you. And if anyone does not have the Spirit of Christ, he does not belong to Christ. But if Christ is in you, your body is dead because of sin, yet your spirit is alive because of righteousness. And if the Spirit of him who raised Jesus from the dead is living in you, he who raised Christ from the dead will also give life to your mortal bodies through his Spirit, who lives in you. Therefore, brothers, we have an obligation—but it is not to the sinful nature, to live according to it. For if you live according to the sinful nature, you will die; but if by the Spirit you put to death the misdeeds of the body, you will live, because those who are led by the Spirit of God are sons of God. (Romans 8:9–14)

Why doesn't the believer have to live under the control of the sinful nature? _____

_____

_____

What is our obligation now that we are in Christ? _____

_____

_____

How does the Holy Spirit help us? _____

_____

_____

MY RESPONSE

1. In what area of your life are you most aware of your struggle with the sinful nature? _____

_____

_____

2. What would it look like for you to apply the benefit of the Cross to this area of your life? _____

_____

_____

*3. What practical reminder would help you to be more aware of your obligation to put the sinful nature to death through the Spirit?*_____

_____

_____

CONCLUSION

An entirely new potential has opened up to us. It is the possibility of saying yes to God and no to the flesh. This blessing brings with it an inevitable responsibility. Since there are now two ways open to the believer—the possibility of saying yes to God or of acting according to the old nature—we have the responsibility of applying the work of the Cross to the flesh. Consequently, Paul not only says that believers have already crucified the sinful nature, he commands them to "put to death" the flesh in their present experience: "Put to death, therefore, whatever belongs to your earthly nature: sexual immorality, impurity, lust, evil desires and greed, which is idolatry" (Colossians 3:5; cf. Romans 8:13–14). The sinful nature can be "put to death," but it cannot be changed. It will never be capable of pleasing God. The sinful nature is incapable of submitting to God or of pleasing Him (Romans 8:6–8). The only way to defeat the continuing presence of sin is to take up the cross.

PRAYER

Thank God for the cross of Christ. Ask Him to help you "reckon" yourself dead to sin.

HANDLING
TEMPTATION

KEY PASSAGE: *And lead us not into temptation, but deliver us from the evil one.*
(Matthew 6:13)

WISE WORDS

Some day, in years to come, you will be wrestling with the great temptation, or trembling under the great sorrow of your life. But the real struggle is here, now in these quiet weeks.
PHILLIPS BROOKS

There are situations which will be dangerous to you; watch and pray, always be on guard lest you fall into temptation.
D. MARTYN LLOYD-JONES

THOUGHT STARTER

When do you feel most vulnerable to temptation? _____

_____

_____

What do you do in such situations? _____

_____

_____

What do you do to protect yourself from temptation? _____

_____

_____

SCRIPTURE STUDY

Christ's work made us free from sin. Read each of the following passages and identify the kind of freedom it describes.

Romans 5:9 _____

Romans 6:12–14 _____

2 Corinthians 5:21 _____

The Scriptures outline three major areas of freedom. First, we are free from the guilt of sin. The guilt that should have been ours has been transferred to Christ. Second, we are free from the divine wrath that is the natural consequence of sin. The Scriptures frequently warn that the deeds of the sinful nature provoke God to anger but Jesus is called the one "who rescues us from the coming wrath" (1 Thessalonians 1:10). Because His death and resurrection have made us righteous in God's sight, we will be spared the wrath that is to come. However, Jesus has done more than give us positional freedom from sin. We also enjoy freedom in a very practical sense. We have been freed from sin's power. It is no longer the ruling force in the believer's life. This is because a spiritual change has taken place. Because of Jesus' death and resurrection, those who have trusted in Him have been made righteous. We now have the freedom to become the righteousness of God, 2 Corinthians 5:21 tells us.

Does freedom from sin's ruling power mean that we should no longer experience temptation once we place our faith in Christ? If not, why not? _____

_____

_____

_____

How did Paul describe his own struggle with sin in Romans 7:15–23? _____

_____

_____

What is Paul referring to when he speaks of "the law of sin" at work in his members? _____

_____

_____

Is Paul saying that sinful behavior is inevitable? _____

_____

_____

Although the presence of the sinful nature makes temptation a very real threat to the Christian, there are practical steps that we can take to deal with it. One of the most effective is to be proactive in our response. We do not need to wait until we are in the midst of temptation before setting up safeguards.

What safeguard does Jesus advise us to take in Matthew 6:13 and 26:41? _____

_____

_____

Is prayer alone sufficient to keep us from experiencing temptation? _____

_____

_____

What other strategy is encouraged in Proverbs 1:15? _____

_____

_____

Woe to the world because of the things that cause people to sin! . . . If your hand or your foot causes you to sin, cut it off and throw it away. It is better for you to enter life maimed or crippled than to have two hands or two feet and be thrown into eternal fire. And if your eye causes you to sin, gouge it out and throw it away. It is better for you to enter life with one eye than to have two eyes and be thrown into the fire of hell. (Matthew 18:7–9)

Can temptation always be avoided? _____

_____

_____

Do you think Jesus expects us to take the commands of this passage literally? If not, what does He really mean?

_____

_____

_____

No temptation has seized you except what is common to man. And God is faithful; he will not let you be tempted beyond what you can bear. But when you are tempted, he will also provide a way out so that you can stand up under it. (1 Corinthians 10:13)

What hope do we have each time we face temptation, according to 1 Corinthians 10:13?

_____

_____

_____

What does this verse say that God will never do?

_____

_____

_____

What will He always do?

_____

_____

How will this help you when you are experiencing temptation?

_____

_____

_____

MY RESPONSE

1. Think of a time when you were tempted but refused to give in. _____

_____

_____

2. How did God provide a way out? _____

_____

_____

3. How did prayer play a role in your victory over sin? _____

_____

_____

4. Think of a time when you gave in to temptation. Can you identify the "way out" that you failed to take advantage of at the time? _____

_____

_____

5. Have you asked God's forgiveness? _____

_____

_____

CONCLUSION

To deal with sin proactively, prayer should be coupled with the commonsense strategy of avoidance. In the Lord's Prayer we pray that God will keep us from those circumstances of temptation that we do not know about. Sometimes, however, we knowingly place ourselves within the range of temptation. Avoiding temptation means that, whenever possible, we will keep away from those circumstances where we know we will be tempted. When others invite us to join them in sin, Proverbs 1:15 advises "do not go along with them, do not set foot on their paths." To accomplish this we may need to replace old interests or friends with new ones. God does not tempt. Nor does He allow the believer to be tempted beyond his or her ability to bear it. Instead, He enables us to endure temptation by providing a way out. Your greatest weapons in the battle against sin may be your own two feet!

PRAYER

Make a list of the areas where you feel most vulnerable to temptation and pray for each one individually. Think of someone else you know and pray that God would keep him or her from temptation.

_____

_____

_____

THE
STAGES OF
TEMPTATION

KEY PASSAGE: *When tempted, no one should say, "God is tempting me." For God cannot be tempted by evil, nor does he tempt anyone; but each one is tempted when, by his own evil desire, he is dragged away and enticed. Then, after desire has conceived, it gives birth to sin; and sin, when it is full-grown, gives birth to death.* (James 1:13–15)

WISE WORDS

It is your greatest honour, and your highest wisdom, peremptorily to withstand the beginnings of a temptation, for an after-remedy comes often too late.
THOMAS BROOKS

Better shun the bait than struggle in the snare.
JOHN DRYDEN

THOUGHT STARTER

When is the best time to resist temptation? _____

_____

_____

Where does temptation come from? _____

_____

_____

When was the last time you were tempted? How did you respond? _____

_____

_____

SCRIPTURE STUDY

James 1:13–15 describes three major stages in temptation. The first is the stage of desire. This is the stage when we feel the draw to sin on two fronts. We are drawn to it internally as we are "dragged away and enticed" by our own evil desire. But we also feel it externally as we are attracted to "the pleasures of sin" (Hebrews 11:25). At this point, although we are attracted to it, we have not acted upon the desire. Like the fisherman's bait that hides the sharp barb of the hook, the attractiveness of sin masks the ultimate disappointment and eventual bondage that is its result.

Where does James say that the desire to sin originates? _____

_____

_____

What does James say is never the source of temptation? _____

_____

_____

Is the appeal of temptation itself a sin? _____

_____

_____

James describes the second stage of temptation as conception: "Then, after desire has conceived, it gives birth to sin" (James 1:15a). During the conception stage, it is not unusual to begin to rationalize the decision to sin. We may reason, for example, that what we are contemplating is only a "small" sin. Of course, there is no such thing. There are no "little" sins.

According to James 2:10, how many sins does it take to make us guilty of violating all of God's Law? _____

_____

_____

Read the passages below. In what sense might the actions described have been viewed as little sins? What was God's view of each?

Moses (Numbers 20:8–12)
Nature of the sin: _____

_____

_____

God's response: _____

_____

_____

Uzzah (1 Chronicles 13:9–10)
Nature of the sin: _____

_____

_____

God's response: _____

_____

_____

Ananias and Sapphira (Acts 5:1–11)

Nature of the sin: _____

_____

_____

God's response: _____

_____

_____

Moses struck the rock instead of speaking to it. To us it seems like a small thing, but in God's eyes it was a failure to honor Him as holy. Uzzah reached out to steady the ark of the covenant when it seemed about to topple from the cart that was transporting it to Jerusalem, and he was struck down. Ananias and Sapphira "fudged" in their accounting to God. They sold a piece of property, kept back part of it for themselves and gave the rest to the church—leaving everyone with the impression that they had given all the proceeds to God. They had lied to the Holy Spirit and were struck dead as a result. There are no "little" sins. When it comes to God's Law, it only takes offending at one point to make us guilty of breaking it all. Our smallest sin was enough to require Christ to suffer and die.

Once sin has conceived, it is not finished. The final stage is one of development and eventual bondage. "Sin, when it is full-grown, gives birth to death" (James 1:15b). Certainly physical death is part of what James has in mind. However, as we have seen, the biblical concept of spiritual death encompasses much more. Sin leads to slavery.

What does Paul say is true of the one who chooses to obey sin, according to Romans 6:16? _____

_____

_____

The three stages in temptation—desire, temptation, and eventual bondage—are on display in the temptation of the first couple. Analyze Satan's temptation of Adam and Eve, described in Genesis 3:1–24. Where do you find these three stages reflected in their experience? _____

_____

_____

Sin always promises more than it can deliver. For proof, we need only look at the first instance of temptation in the Garden of Eden. Satan promised Eve that if she ate the fruit, she would "be like God, knowing good and evil" (Genesis 3:5). This appeal was strengthened further by the fact that it was rooted in legitimate desires and normal appetites. Deceived by Satan's false promises, however, Eve lost sight of God's warning that disobedience would result in death.

MY RESPONSE

James compares the appeal of temptation to the fisherman's bait that hides a sharp hook. The initial attractiveness of temptation masks the ultimate disappointment and eventual bondage that is the result of sin. Think of a common temptation you face.

1. What is its attraction? _____

_____

_____

2. What is the "hook"? _____

_____

_____

3. What practical steps can you take to avoid this temptation? _____

_____

_____

CONCLUSION

Today's "little" sin paves the way for tomorrow's bondage. It may be conceived in momentary pleasure, but it will produce a harvest of regret. What began as an occasional "mistake" quickly develops into a practice. That practice eventually becomes a habit of life. Why do some who profess to be Christ's disciples live as though they are slaves to sin? It is not because they have to. In fact, they are commanded not to. It is because they offer themselves to the flesh in voluntary slavery. It is time for them to discover that they have been serving a corpse. All who would be Christ's disciples must bear the cross. Yet all who do find, to their eternal joy, that it is really the cross that bears them.

PRAYER

Pray about the temptation mentioned above. Thank God for His protection and deliverance from it in the past. Ask for His help in avoiding it in the future.

THE
OBLIGATIONS OF
DISCIPLESHIP

JESUS,
OUR EXAMPLE

KEY PASSAGE: *A student is not above his teacher, but everyone who is fully trained will be like his teacher.* (Luke 6:40)

WISE WORDS

Our pattern is still above us; the best of men are ashamed when they compare their lives to the life of Christ. A vain heart may swell with pride when a man compares himself with other men . . . but if any man will compare his life with Christ's, he will find abundant cause to be humbled.
JOHN FLAVEL

Ordinary people in common surroundings can live from the abundance of God's kingdom, letting the spirit and the actions of Jesus be the natural outflow from their lives.
DALLAS WILLARD

THOUGHT STARTER

Who is the most Christlike person you have ever known? _____

_____

_____

What was it about him or her that made you think of Christ? _____

_____

_____

SCRIPTURE STUDY

Jesus is our Savior, but He is also our example. The desire to avoid a works-oriented approach to the Christian life has caused many evangelicals to ignore Christ's role as a model for the believer. Instead of trying to be like Jesus, we have adopted a far more modest goal. We are content to be "sort of" like Jesus. We hold Christ's life as a beautiful but unrealistic ideal. In fact, if another believer were to tell us that he or she actually lived like Christ, we would suspect that the person was either exaggerating or conclude he or she had a serious problem with spiritual pride. We want to be like Jesus, but we do not think that it is really possible. Yet Jesus taught that those who were genuinely interested in being His disciples would follow His example.

Read Luke 6:39–46. Then answer the following questions.

What was the main point of Jesus' account of the blind man? _____

_____

_____

What is the blind man unable to do? _____

_____

_____

What will happen to those who try to follow the blind man? _____

_____

_____

Who do you think the blind man is supposed to represent in this parable? _____

_____

_____

What will be true of those who follow such teachers? Why? _____

_____

_____

In Matthew's account of this saying (see Matthew 15:14), the "blind man" refers to the Pharisees and teachers of the Law who are "blind guides." The parable is a warning not to imitate their example and teaching. A student will become like the teacher he or she follows. One who follows a blind leader is liable to end up in a ditch. Luke's version highlights the alternative. Christ's disciples should avoid the example of blind guides like these religious leaders and imitate Christ.

How do the verses below illustrate Jesus' criticism that the Pharisees and teachers of the Law were like someone who attempts to remove a speck of sawdust from the eye of another while ignoring the "plank" in his own eye?

Matthew 23:1–12 _____

_____

Matthew 23:13–23 _____

_____

Matthew 23:24–26 _____

_____

Matthew 23:27–28 _____

_____

The Pharisees were the descendants of those who had resisted the influence of Greek culture in the period between the Old and New Testaments. They had a reputation for being scrupulous in their observance of the Law of Moses. Although relatively few in number compared to the rest of the population, they were very influential and highly regarded as models of righteousness. Jesus, however, criticized the Pharisees for expecting more of others than they did of themselves and for being more concerned about appearances than about truly righteous behavior.

According to Luke 6:46, what must be true of those who claim Jesus as their "Lord"? _____

_____

_____

How do Philippians 2:12–13 and Colossians 1:27–29 help you to understand how this can be a reality? _____

_____

_____

What do these verses have in common with Jesus' statement about the tree being known by its fruit in Luke 6:44?

_____

_____

_____

As disciples, our goal is not to "measure up" to the life of Christ but to "work out" the reality of the Christ who lives in us. This standard is not something outside of us; it is a principle that resides within. It is "Christ in you, the hope of glory" (Colossians 1:27). There is effort involved, but it is an effort that has been energized by the life of Christ. The apostle Paul's practice of imitating Christ was rooted in his confidence that God was already at work in him. He was not trying to "catch up" to Christ but had himself already been "taken hold of" by Christ. "Not that I have already obtained all this, or have already been made perfect, but I press on to take hold of that for which Christ Jesus took hold of me. Brothers, I do not consider myself yet to have taken hold of it. But one thing I do: Forgetting what is behind and straining toward what is ahead, I press on toward the goal to win the prize for which God has called me heavenward in Christ Jesus" (Philippians 3:12–14). The responsibility is ours, but the power to comply comes from God.

Dear friends, now we are children of God, and what we will be has not yet been made known. But we know that when he appears, we shall be like him, for we shall see him as he is. Everyone who has this hope in him purifies himself, just as he is pure. (1 John 3:2–3)

What confidence does John say that we have as we follow Christ's example? _____

_____

_____

How should this certainty affect us in daily living? _____

_____

_____

In this way, love is made complete among us so that we will have confidence on the day of judgment, because in this world we are like him. (1 John 4:17)

What value does Christlikeness have on the day of judgment? _____

_____

_____

MY RESPONSE

Three New Testament passages command us to imitate Christ in some way. Using the following chart, in each passage identify the aspect of Christ's life that you are to imitate and note one area of your life where this characteristic is needed and one specific way you can begin to imitate Christ.

	Aspect of Christ's Life	Area in My Life Where I Need This	Way I Can Imitate Christ
Ephesians 5:1–2			
Hebrews 12:1–3			
1 Peter 1:14–16			

CONCLUSION

God's standard for the disciple's life is Christ. He is the mark by which our spiritual maturity is measured and the aim of all our training. The reason that God has given believers spiritual gifts is to build the church up "until we all reach unity in the faith and in the knowledge of the Son of God and become mature, *attaining to the whole measure of the fullness of Christ*" (Ephesians 4:13; italics added). Our ultimate hope as believers is that we will one day be like Christ: We must wait until Christ appears to be fully like Him, but this does not mean that we should wait until then before expecting to see some resemblance. The discipleship experience is training in Christlikeness.

PRAYER

Is there an area of your life that you would like to see brought into greater conformity to Christ? Take a few minutes to pray about it now. Ask God to work through His Word and the Holy Spirit to produce Christlikeness in your life in this area.

l e s s o n   t w o

THE
OBLIGATION
OF HUMILITY

KEY PASSAGE: *Do nothing out of selfish ambition or vain conceit, but in humility consider others better than yourselves. Each of you should look not only to your own interests, but also to the interests of others.* (Philippians 2:3–4)

WISE WORDS

There is something in humility which strangely exalts the heart.

AUGUSTINE

Do not imagine that if you meet a really humble man he will be what most people call "humble" nowadays: he will not be a sort of greasy, smarmy person, who is always telling you that, of course, he is nobody. Probably all you will think about him is that he seemed a cheerful, intelligent chap who took a real interest in what you said to him.

C. S. LEWIS

THOUGHT STARTER

How would you define humility? _____

_____

_____

What is the difference between true and false humility? _____

_____

_____

What does true humility look like in your life? _____

_____

_____

SCRIPTURE STUDY

Humility is an essential precondition for discipleship because a disciple ultimately is one who is under the yoke of Christ. Unfortunately, humility is not highly valued, even by many Christians. Today's culture favors pride, which is considered to be an asset rather than a liability. If humility is appreciated at all, it tends to be admired from a distance. We may approve of another's humility but do not often seek it for ourselves. Yet the follower of Christ has been called to humility.

Come to me, all you who are weary and burdened, and I will give you rest. Take my yoke upon you and learn from me, for I am gentle and humble in heart, and you will find rest for your souls. For my yoke is easy and my burden is light. (Matthew 11:28–30)

Why do you think Jesus used the image of a yoke to describe the disciple's relationship to Him? _____

_____

_____

What does He expect of those who accept His yoke? _____

_____

_____

What does He promise to those who take up His yoke? _____

_____

_____

Jesus says, "My yoke is easy." What other "yoke" might we take upon ourselves instead of the one Jesus wants us to bear? _____

_____

_____

How does Luke 11:46 say that Christ's yoke of discipleship differs from the kinds of burdens the religious leaders of His day placed upon their disciples? _____

_____

_____

Read again the key passage, Philippians 2:3–4. Then answer the following questions.

What does Paul identify as the opposite of humility? _____

_____

_____

What does he say is the mark of true humility? _____

_____

_____

Paul's command is troubling to some because it seems to say that we must run ourselves down in order to be humble; we are to consider everyone else to be better than we are. Is a low self-image really the key to biblical humility? Not really. False humility is also a form of pride. The person who is always hanging his head and has nothing good to say about himself is usually more prideful than the person who graciously accepts a compliment. False humility is marked by two primary characteristics mentioned in Philippians 2:3–4. The first is something the apostle calls "selfish ambition." This is the desire to advance my own interests at the expense of others. It is the competitive spirit twisted by the self-absorption of the sinful nature. The other mark of pride is "vain conceit." This is an attitude that is rooted in a false estimation of one's position. It amounts to an empty boast. In false humility this kind of conceit is reflected in the denial of real accomplishments or true ability. The person who achieves a difficult goal and then says that it was "nothing" isn't being humble. He or she is being untruthful.

In what ways does Paul's description of himself in the following passages reflect an attitude of humility?

1 Corinthians 15:3–10 _____

_____

2 Corinthians 11:17–30 _____

_____

Why aren't Paul's statements regarding his accomplishments examples of prideful boasting? _____

_____

_____

According to 2 Corinthians 12:7–12, why did God allow Paul to be afflicted by a "thorn in the flesh"? _____

_____

_____

What did Paul ask God to do? What was the answer to his prayer? _____

_____

_____

How did God's reply affect Paul's view of himself and his circumstances? _____

_____

_____

MY RESPONSE

1. Make a list of some of the things that God's grace has enabled you to accomplish. _____

_____

_____

2. How do these accomplishments highlight God's ability to use you despite your weakness? _____

_____

_____

CONCLUSION

It is said that when Queen Victoria lay dying, a member of the royal household wondered aloud whether she would be happy in heaven. "I don't know," the queen's son replied, "She will have to walk behind the angels—and she won't like that!" The test of true humility, however, does not lie in our ability to walk behind the angels so much as it does in our willingness to look out for the interests of others and to give place to them. It is not surprising, then, that along with humility another mark of the disciple is the willingness to submit.

PRAYER

Where do you sense God wants to demonstrate His power through your weakness today? Ask God to reveal Himself in that area today.

THE
OBLIGATION
OF SUBMISSION

KEY PASSAGE: *Submit to one another out of reverence for Christ.*
(Ephesians 5:21)

WISE WORDS

To man's authority we may be subject in respect of the outward man in things lawful. But for our souls and consciences, we have no fathers and masters, but only our Father and Master in heaven.
SAMUEL BOLTON

God has so bound us to each other, that no man ought to avoid subjection. And where love reigns, there is mutual servitude. I do not except even kings and governors, for they rule that they may serve.
JOHN CALVIN

THOUGHT STARTER

Whose authority are you under? _____

_____

_____

To whom do you find it easy to submit? Why? _____

_____

_____

To whom do you find it most difficult to submit? Why? _____

_____

_____

SCRIPTURE STUDY

If humility is low on society's wish list of character traits, the practice of submission is even lower. In an age of equal rights, the practice of submission has become synonymous with weakness and oppression. Christ's example, however, is proof that submission does not necessarily imply inferiority. When Jesus chose to submit to the Father's will, He was not any less the Son of God, nor was He any less equal with the Father in nature and power. In the same way, when disciples follow Christ's pattern of submission they are not any less than those to whom they submit.

How do the following passages illustrate Jesus' practice of submission?

Luke 2:51 _____

_____

Matthew 17:24–27 _____

_____

Matthew 20:20–23 _____

_____

John 5:30 _____

_____

Mark 14:32–36 _____

_____

1 Corinthians 15:25–28 _____

_____

Read Philippians 2:5–11. Then answer the following questions.

How does Paul describe Christ's position in these verses? _____

_____

_____

What does he say that Christ did not do? What did He do instead? _____

_____

_____

How did this act of submission to the Father's will affect Christ during the Incarnation? _____

_____

_____

What will be its end result? _____

_____

_____

What does Paul mean when he says that our attitude should be the same as that of Christ Jesus? _____

_____

_____

Read Romans 13:1–7. Then answer the following questions.

According to Paul, to whom does the Bible call us to submit and under what kinds of circumstances? _____
_____
_____

What does he say is God's purpose in this? _____
_____
_____

Restate the principle of verse 7 in your own words. _____
_____
_____

All believers are commanded to submit to "the governing authorities." The context indicates that civil government is in view, and the plural suggests that Christians must answer to multiple levels of authority. The primary role of civil government is to keep order and punish evildoers. Christians have a responsibility to support those in authority by paying their taxes.

Read 1 Peter 2:13–17. The passage not only tells us who to submit to but also provides a motive for our submission and describes the manner in which it should be carried out.

Why should we submit? _____
_____
_____

What should our attitude be as we submit? _____
_____
_____

What additional motive is given in Hebrews 13:17? _____
_____
_____

When is it wrong to submit to authority, according to Acts 5:27–29? _____
_____
_____

Submit to one another out of reverence for Christ. (Ephesians 5:21)

THE OBLIGATION OF SUBMISSION 63

What motive does Paul give for submitting to one another? _____

_____

_____

The obligation to submit is mutual in the body of Christ. Nobody is exempt. Those who are in positions of authority practice a form of submission by leading in a way that is sensitive to the needs and concerns of those who are under them. They have authority, but it is the authority to serve. Or as John Calvin put it, "They rule that they may serve."

Wives, submit to your husbands as to the Lord. For the husband is the head of the wife as Christ is the head of the church, his body, of which he is the Savior. (Ephesians 5:22–23)

What kind of leadership does Paul tell Christian husbands to exercise in Ephesians 5:25–29? _____

_____

_____

What kind of submission does Paul call for in Ephesians 5:33? _____

_____

_____

Children, obey your parents in the Lord, for this is right. "Honor your father and mother"—which is the first commandment with a promise—"that it may go well with you and that you may enjoy long life on the earth." (Ephesians 6:1–3)

What does the phrase "in the Lord" imply? _____

_____

_____

Submit yourselves, then, to God. Resist the devil, and he will flee from you. (James 4:7)

Under what difficult circumstances were New Testament believers expected to submit in the following passages?

Colossians 3:22 _____

_____

1 Peter 2:18–25 _____

_____

MY RESPONSE

Look again at the list of those to whom you must submit. In practical terms, what should your submission look like? _____

_____

_____

CONCLUSION

In the church's relationships, submission is more properly a gift to be offered than a right to be demanded. Although equal with the Father, Jesus did not cling to that equality. His submission was voluntary. He "made Himself nothing" (Philippians 2:7). In the Incarnation, Jesus "emptied" or stripped Himself of the prerogatives that were His by virtue of His divine nature. He was not compelled to do this by the Father. He freely took it upon Himself. During His earthly ministry Christ chose not to exercise His equality and instead took upon Himself the role of a servant. According to the writer of Hebrews, He "learned obedience" during this period (Hebrews 5:8).

PRAYER

Pray for those who are in authority over you and for yourself as you submit to them.

THE
OBLIGATION
OF PATIENCE

KEY PASSAGE: *Be completely humble and gentle; be patient, bearing with one another in love.*
(Ephesians 4:2)

WISE WORDS

All men commend patience, although few be willing to practice it.
THOMAS 'A KEMPIS

Patience is not passive; on the contrary, it is active; it is concentrated strength.
EDWARD G. BULWER-LYTTON

THOUGHT STARTER

Describe a time when you showed patience to another person. What did you do? _____

_____

_____

Did you find it easy or difficult? _____

_____

_____

What enabled you to be patient? _____

_____

_____

What role did your faith have in the experience? _____

_____

_____

SCRIPTURE STUDY

Another way disciples are to reflect Christ is by imitating His example of patience. The Scriptures command, "We who are strong ought to bear with the failings of the weak and not to please ourselves. Each of us should please his neighbor for his good, to build him up. For even Christ did not please himself but, as it is written: 'The insults of those who insult you have fallen on me'" (Romans 15:1–3). Based on this passage, answer the following questions.

Who has an obligation to be patient and to whom is this patience to be expressed? _____

_____

_____

What motive does Paul give for being patient with the failings of others? _____

_____

_____

How did Christ provide an example of this in the following passages?

Mark 2:2–12 _____

_____

Mark 5:1–20 _____

_____

Mark 6:31–34 _____

_____

Mark 9:14–30 _____

_____

Luke 23:33–34 _____

_____

John 3:1–12 _____

_____

Or do you show contempt for the riches of his kindness, tolerance and patience, not realizing that God's kindness leads you toward repentance? (Romans 2:4)

How should God's patience affect us, according to the preceding verse? _____

_____

_____

According to the following passages, how do we acquire patience?

Proverbs 19:11 _____

_____

Galatians 5:22–23 _____

_____

Colossians 1:10–12 _____

_____

Colossians 3:12–13 _____

_____

Read Romans 14:1–21. Then answer the following questions.

What practical example of patience does Paul give in these verses? _____

_____

_____

How do verses 10–12 help ease the anxiety we might feel as we show patience to others? _____

_____

_____

How far was Paul willing to go in showing patience to the weaker believer? _____

_____

_____

MY RESPONSE

1. Write the name of at least one person to whom God is calling you to show patience. How do you need to show patience to this individual? _____

_____

_____

2. Why is it important for you to be patient with this person? _____

_____

_____

3. Where do you need God's help most in accomplishing this? _____

_____

_____

CONCLUSION

Our obligation to show patience to others grows out of our own experience. God showed patience when He sent His son to suffer and die on our behalf. He continues to show patience to us on a daily basis. However, patience involves more than merely putting up with others. Biblical patience is patience with a purpose. Our aim in showing patience is to build others up in the faith.

PRAYER

Think of an instance where God showed patience to you. Thank Him for His grace.

l e s s o n   f i v e

THE
OBLIGATION
OF GENEROSITY

KEY PASSAGE: *But just as you excel in everything—in faith, in speech, in knowledge, in complete earnestness and in your love for us —see that you also excel in this grace of giving.*
(2 Corinthians 8:7)

WISE WORDS

Mercy is not just the absence of avarice, but the presence of generosity. More than just 'not being greedy,' it is proactive in giving—not simply giving up wealth but giving out to the needy. As William F. May wrote, "The true opposite of the tight-fistedness of avarice is not the empty-handedness of death, but the open- handedness of love."

OS GUINNESS

Covetousness makes a man miserable, because riches are not means to make a man happy.
JEREMY TAYLOR

THOUGHT STARTER

Describe the most generous thing anyone has ever done for you. _____
_____
_____

What made this action generous—and what prompted it? _____
_____
_____

How did it make you feel? _____
_____
_____

Describe the most generous thing you have done for someone else. _____
_____
_____

What made the action generous—and what prompted it? _____

_____

_____

How did it make you feel? _____

_____

_____

SCRIPTURE STUDY

"Be careful not to do your 'acts of righteousness' before men, to be seen by them. If you do, you will have no reward from your Father in heaven. So when you give to the needy, do not announce it with trumpets, as the hypocrites do in the synagogues and on the streets, to be honored by men. I tell you the truth, they have received their reward in full. But when you give to the needy, do not let your left hand know what your right hand is doing, so that your giving may be in secret. Then your Father, who sees what is done in secret, will reward you." (Matthew 6:1–4)

What motive does Jesus warn His disciples to avoid when giving to others? _____

_____

_____

What does He say is wrong with this kind of giving? _____

_____

_____

How did this motive show itself in the practices of those who made charitable donations in Jesus' day? _____

_____

_____

How might we give and "announce it with trumpets" today? _____

_____

_____

According to Jesus, the searching question that distinguishes true generosity from hypocritical giving is, "Why am I being generous?" If my motive is to be noticed by others, then my giving springs from a hypocritical rather than a generous spirit. This kind of giving is driven by a selfish desire to be seen and praised by others rather than by a genuine concern for the needs of others. Its purpose is to bring glory to myself rather than God. In a sense, when I give in order to be seen by others, I am really giving to myself.

How can we avoid hypocritical giving? _____

_____

_____

What do you think Jesus meant when He said not to let your left hand know what your right hand is doing when being generous? _____

_____

_____

"No one can serve two masters. Either he will hate the one and love the other, or he will be devoted to the one and despise the other. You cannot serve both God and Money." (Matthew 6:24)

What does money have to do with discipleship? _____

_____

_____

Money and our relationship to it is very much a matter of discipleship. Jesus warned that it is impossible to serve both God and money (Matthew 6:24; Luke 16:13). In view of this, we should not view giving as an optional aspect of our worship. According to Jesus, the way we relate to our wealth and our possessions is a litmus test of our true devotion. It is an "either/or" proposition. Either we serve God or we serve money. We cannot be devoted to both.

Jesus sat down opposite the place where the offerings were put and watched the crowd putting their money into the temple treasury. Many rich people threw in large amounts. But a poor widow came and put in two very small copper coins, worth only a fraction of a penny. Calling his disciples to him, Jesus said, "I tell you the truth, this poor widow has put more into the treasury than all the others. They all gave out of their wealth; but she, out of her poverty, put in everything—all she had to live on." (Mark 12:41–44)

Compare the widow's offering to the others that were placed into the temple treasury. How did it differ?

Widow's Offering	**Other Offerings**
_____	_____
_____	_____
_____	_____

Do you find anything surprising about her action? _____

_____

_____

What does this indicate about the standard God uses to evaluate our giving? _____

_____

_____

We have different gifts, according to the grace given us. If a man's gift is prophesying, let him use it in proportion to his faith. If it is serving, let him serve; if it is teaching, let him teach; if it is encouraging, let him encourage; if it is contributing to the needs of others, let him give generously; if it is leadership, let him govern diligently; if it is showing mercy, let him do it cheerfully. (Romans 12:6–8)

In Romans 12:8 Paul indicates that some Christians have the spiritual gift of giving to others. Does this mean that those who have a different gift do not need to give? If not, why? _____

_____

_____

Does having the spiritual gift of giving automatically guarantee that you will be generous? _____

_____

_____

Read 2 Corinthians 8:1–24. Then answer the following questions.

What was surprising about the giving of the Macedonian churches? _____

_____

_____

Were the Corinthians obligated to contribute as well? _____

_____

_____

Why did Paul want them to take part in this offering? _____

_____

_____

What does Paul imply when he describes giving as a "grace"? _____

_____

_____

For you know the grace of our Lord Jesus Christ, that though he was rich, yet for your sakes he became poor, so that you through his poverty might become rich. (2 Corinthians 8:9)

In what sense has Christ made us "rich"? _____

_____

_____

How should Christ's example motivate us to be generous? _____

_____

_____

MY RESPONSE

1. Think of at least one concrete way to demonstrate the grace of generosity in each of the following areas:

At home _____

_____

At church _____

_____

At work _____

_____

In the neighborhood _____

_____

2. Choose one of the areas above and make plans to implement your idea.

To whom will you show generosity? _____

_____

_____

How will you do it? _____

_____

_____

When will you begin? _____

_____

_____

CONCLUSION

The disciple who excels in the grace of giving is marked by a generous spirit that does not limit its giving to the Sunday offering. Those who have a generous spirit are generous with their time, their words, and their efforts. They do not give grudgingly but experience a sense of joy when God gives them an opportunity to be generous. The poet John Donne rightly observed, "There is only one charity, to do all, all that we can."

PRAYER

Ask God to help you excel in the "grace of giving" today and to give you an opportunity to carry out the plan you have outlined above.

THE
DYNAMICS OF
SPIRITUAL LIFE

WHAT IS "SPIRITUALITY"?

KEY PASSAGE: *Dear friends, do not believe every spirit, but test the spirits to see whether they are from God, because many false prophets have gone out into the world.*
(1 John 4:1)

WISE WORDS

The resurrection theory requires us to accept that a human being is a purely physical object, a biochemical machine completely and exhaustively described by the known laws of physics. There are no mysterious "vital" forces. More generally, it requires us to regard a "person" as a particular (very complicated) type of computer program: the human "soul" is nothing but a specific program being run on a computing machine called the brain.

FRANK J. TIPLER

What then is the end of all? Each part of man returns to his original source—his body to the earth as it was; the spirit—to God of whom it is, and who gave it. And where now is the spirit found? In unconscious slumber of the grave? Far from it. It returns to God—home whence it came—to "the Father of spirits," who claims it for himself.

CHARLES BRIDGES

THOUGHT STARTER

What differences can you see reflected in the two quotes above? _____

_____

_____

Which one do you think is more accurate? Why? _____

_____

_____

What do we usually mean when we say that someone is a "spiritual" person? _____

_____

_____

Is everyone "spiritual"? _____

_____

_____

SCRIPTURE STUDY

There's a high level of interest in spirituality today, and media reports attest to its various forms, which range from the championship professional basketball coach who uses Buddhist principles to help him get the best out of his team to the best-selling author and motivational speaker who draws on Eastern mysticism for the spiritual "laws" that lead to personal success. Many viewers watch popular TV shows about the everyday adventures of angels, demons, vampires, and spirits.

No wonder most people tend to define spirituality in personal rather than in biblical terms. This means that our notion of what it means to be spiritual is usually reduced to a mystical experience. Yet the Scriptures warn us that we have an obligation to test our "spiritual" experiences.

Read 1 John 4:1–6. Then answer the following questions.

What important warning does John give in this passage? _____

_____

_____

Why, according to John, aren't all spiritual experiences equally valid? _____

_____

_____

How can one tell whether God is the ultimate source of a spiritual experience? _____

_____

_____

The apostle's warning in these verses is based upon two important assumptions. The first assumption is that spiritual experiences are not self-validating. The mere fact that someone has had a spiritual experience does not guarantee that God was the source. There are spirits that do not come from God and do not acknowledge Jesus Christ. A second important assumption is that it is possible to have a genuine spiritual experience that does not originate with God. In order to understand how this is possible, we need to know how our capacity for spiritual experiences first originated.

This is the account of the heavens and the earth when they were created. When the LORD God made the earth and the heavens . . . the LORD God formed the man from the dust of the ground and breathed into his nostrils the breath of life, and the man became a living being. (Genesis 2:4–7)

How did our spiritual nature originate? _____

_____

_____

What does the Bible say that man became after God gave him the "breath of life"? _____

_____

_____

The origin of mankind's spiritual nature is described in Genesis 2:7, which says that "the LORD God formed the man from the dust of the ground and breathed into his nostrils the breath of life, and the man became a living being." The spirit is what animates man and makes him "a living being." It is significant that both the Hebrew and the Greek terms for spirit can also be translated "breath." The human spirit comes from the "breath" of God. He is called "the Father of spirits" (Hebrews 12:9).

For who among men knows the thoughts of a man except the man's spirit within him? In the same way no one knows the thoughts of God except the Spirit of God. (1 Corinthians 2:11)

What is one of the functions of the "spirit," according to this verse? _____

_____

_____

Does this verse imply that Christians are the only ones who possess a spiritual nature? _____

_____

_____

In this verse Paul implies that every human being has a spiritual nature. The spirit is that part of us that dwells on our innermost thoughts. Paul also implies that the spirit is active even in those who are "spiritually dead." The implied answer to the question "Who among men knows the thoughts of a man except the man's spirit within him?" is "Nobody." Everybody has a functioning spirit in the sense spoken of in this verse. We might call this first level of spirituality a state of ordinary spirituality.

We have not received the spirit of the world but the Spirit who is from God, that we may understand what God has freely given us. This is what we speak, not in words taught us by human wisdom but in words taught by the Spirit, expressing spiritual truths in spiritual words. The man without the Spirit does not accept the things that come from the Spirit of God, for they are foolishness to him, and he cannot understand them, because they are spiritually discerned. The spiritual man makes judgments about all things, but he himself is not subject to any man's judgment: "For who has known the mind of the Lord that he may instruct him?" But we have the mind of Christ. (1 Corinthians 2:12–16)

How does the spiritual nature of the Christian differ from that of the ordinary person? _____

_____

_____

What does Paul say is impossible for the person who does not possess the Holy Spirit? _____

_____

_____

In view of this, what would you say is the primary difference between ordinary spirituality and Christian spirituality? _____

_____

_____

Believers and unbelievers alike possess a spiritual nature. The thing that sets the Christian apart from the non-Christian is the presence of the Holy Spirit. Because of the ministry of the Holy Spirit, the Christian is able to understand and accept the things taught by the Spirit. Those who do not possess the Holy Spirit cannot accept these truths. They seem like foolishness to them. This severely limits the unbeliever's spiritual potential. The unbeliever possesses a spirit and is capable of having spiritual experiences, but he or she is not capable of responding to God. This helps us to understand why today's popular interest in spirituality does not also bring with it a corresponding interest in Christ. It is one-sided spirituality that is open only to spiritual experiences that do not originate with God.

MY RESPONSE

1. Can you think of a time when you had a "spiritual" experience prior to trusting in Christ? What was its source? _____

_____

_____

2. How do you know that your spiritual experiences emanate from the Spirit of truth rather than the spirit of falsehood? _____

_____

_____

3. What role does the Holy Spirit play in your own spiritual life? _____

_____

_____

CONCLUSION

The fact that everyone has a spiritual nature means that spirituality is not an exclusively Christian concept. However, the Bible warns us to be on guard in this area because not every spiritual experience originates with God. Those who do not know Christ as Savior lack spiritual life and are unable to accept the things that come of God's Spirit. Those who have trusted in Christ have the mind of Christ.

PRAYER

Thank God for the presence of the Holy Spirit and for the evidence of His ministry in your life.

l e s s o n   t w o

SPIRITUAL
DEATH

KEY PASSAGE: *As for you, you were dead in your transgressions and sins, in which you used to live when you followed the ways of this world and of the ruler of the kingdom of the air, the spirit who is now at work in those who are disobedient.*
(Ephesians 2:1–2)

WISE WORDS

This is the true account of that host of excuses, which so many make "with one consent." Some have no learning, some have no time. Some are oppressed with business, and the care of money, and some with poverty. Some have difficulties in their own families, and some in their own health. Some have peculiar obstacles in their calling, which others, we are told, cannot understand; and others have peculiar drawbacks at home, and they wait to have them removed. But God has a shorter word in the Bible which describes all these people at once. He says, They are dead.

J. C. RYLE

As spiritual death is nothing else than the alienation of the soul from God, we are all born dead, and we live dead until we are made partakers of the life of Christ.

JOHN CALVIN

THOUGHT STARTER

What does it mean to be "dead" in the physical sense? _____

_____

_____

In what ways is spiritual death like physical death? _____

_____

_____

How does it differ? _____

_____

_____

SCRIPTURE STUDY

One does not need to be a Christian to be interested in spirituality or even to have spiritual experiences. However, although everyone has a spiritual nature, it is a nature that has been damaged by sin. Ephesians 2:1–3 characterizes our spiritual condition prior to trusting in Christ as a state of spiritual death.

As for you, you were dead in your transgressions and sins, in which you used to live when you followed the ways of this world and of the ruler of the kingdom of the air, the spirit who is now at work in those who are disobedient. All of us also lived among them at one time, gratifying the cravings of our sinful nature and following its desires and thoughts. Like the rest, we were by nature objects of wrath.

In what sense were we "dead"? _____

_____

_____

What was our spiritual life like when we were apart from Christ? _____

_____

_____

How did this affect our behavior? _____

_____

_____

How did it affect our relationship with God? _____

_____

_____

Those who are spiritually dead are still spiritually active. They follow "the spirit now at work in those who are disobedient." They are controlled by the sinful nature and respond to its desires and thoughts. To be spiritually dead is to be dead "in trespasses and sins."

Read Romans 5:12–15. Then answer the following questions.

How did spiritual death enter the human race? _____

_____

_____

What do you think Paul means when he says that "death reigned"? _____

_____

_____

God gave the Law of Moses to make us conscious of sin and of our need for forgiveness (cf. Romans 3:20). What, according to Romans 5:13–14, was the indisputable proof that everyone has been affected by Adam's disobedience even prior to the giving of the Law? _____

_____

_____

Read Genesis 2:16–17; 5:5. Then answer the following questions.

When did God say that Adam would die? _____

_____

_____

When does Genesis 5:5 say that he died physically? _____

_____

_____

Read Genesis 3:6–13. Then answer the following questions.

How did Adam and Eve's relationship to God change once they had sinned? _____

_____

_____

How did sin affect their relationship to one another? _____

_____

_____

The Lord warned Adam that when (literally "in the day") he ate of that tree, he would "surely die" (Genesis 2:17). Adam disobeyed, was expelled from the garden, had sons and daughters, and altogether lived for 930 years (Genesis 5:5). Spiritually, however, Adam died the moment he ate of the forbidden tree.

The effects of Adam's disobedience were so far-reaching that we still suffer from them today. When Adam sinned, he did not sin for himself alone. He was serving as our representative. When he disobeyed, his sin was credited to our account, so that in God's eyes "all sinned" (Romans 5:12). In this way, Adam became the source of spiritual death for all humanity. From that moment on, the human race began a downward spiral that removed the possibility of real communion with God and left us destructively self-centered.

Read Romans 1:18–23 and answer these two questions:

Did Adam's descendants lose their interest in spiritual experiences? _____

_____

_____

How did sin affect the spiritual life of Adam's descendants? _____

_____

_____

Adam's descendants did not lose interest in spiritual experiences or their capacity to worship. Religious practice continued after Adam and Eve sinned. The first murder ever committed was sparked by Cain's resentment when God accepted Abel's offering and rejected his (Genesis 4:3–8). But human nature already had been fundamentally altered as a result of Adam's sin. The theologians have used the phrase "total depravity" to describe human nature's fallen state. This does not mean that every person is as bad as he or she can be, but that sin has affected every part of our human nature. Our best acts are stained by sin. Likewise, apart from the intervention of Christ, our interests, desires, and even our worship are inclined to move us away from God.

MY RESPONSE

1. In each of the following areas, describe how spiritual death affected you prior to trusting in Christ.

Body: _____

_____

_____

Mind: _____

_____

_____

Emotions: _____

_____

_____

Spirit: _____

_____

_____

2. What was your spiritual life like when you were still dead in your transgressions and sins? _____

_____

_____

3. How did this condition affect your relationship to others? _____

_____

_____

4. How did it affect your relationship to God? _____
_____
_____

CONCLUSION

Unlike physical death, which leaves the body inactive, those who are spiritually dead continue to be spiritually active but are dead to God and unable to respond to Him. This is the universal condition of everyone who does not know Jesus Christ as Savior. The only remedy for spiritual death is the spiritual life that comes through faith in Christ. Those who trust in Christ receive forgiveness and eternal life and are no longer spiritually dead.

PRAYER

If you have never placed your faith in Jesus Christ for eternal life, ask Him to grant you spiritual life. If you have, identify at least one major change that has taken place in your life as a result and thank Him for it.

lesson three

SPIRITUAL
LIFE

KEY PASSAGE: *But because of his great love for us, God, who is rich in mercy, made us alive with Christ even when we were dead in transgressions—it is by grace you have been saved.*
(Ephesians 2:4–5)

WISE WORDS

The sages have a hundred maps to give
That trace their crawling cosmos like a tree,
They rattle reason out through many a sieve
That stores the sand and lets the gold go free;
And all these things are less than dust to me
Because my name is Lazarus and I live.

G. K. CHESTERTON

The cross makes us whole; not all at once indeed, but it does the work effectually. Before we reached it we were not "whole," but broken and scattered, without a center toward which to gravitate. The cross forms that center, and in doing so, it draws together the disordered fragments of our being; it "unites our heart" (Psalm 86:11), producing wholeness or unity that no object of less powerful attractiveness could accomplish.

HORATIUS BONAR

THOUGHT STARTER

What would you say to someone who claimed that the Christian life was simply a matter of turning over a new leaf? _____

_____

_____

Do you know anyone whose life changed significantly after trusting in Christ? How did that person change?

_____

_____

_____

To what did the person attribute the change? _____

_____

_____

SCRIPTURE STUDY

No condition is worse than that of spiritual death. Fortunately, God did not leave us in this helpless state. Jesus Christ came so that we might have "life to the full" (John 10:10). If "ordinary" spirituality is a state of spiritual death, the most important distinctive of Christian spirituality is that it is a state of spiritual life.

But because of his great love for us, God, who is rich in mercy, made us alive with Christ even when we were dead in transgressions—it is by grace you have been saved. And God raised us up with Christ and seated us with him in the heavenly realms in Christ Jesus, in order that in the coming ages he might show the incomparable riches of his grace, expressed in his kindness to us in Christ Jesus. For it is by grace you have been saved, through faith—and this not from yourselves, it is the gift of God—not by works, so that no one can boast. For we are God's workmanship, created in Christ Jesus to do good works, which God prepared in advance for us to do. (Ephesians 2:4–10)

What motivated God to give us new life? _____

_____

_____

How did He do this? _____

_____

_____

What does Paul say is true of us now that we are in Christ? _____

_____

_____

How does this new life affect us? _____

_____

_____

Compare Ephesians 2:1–3 with Ephesians 2:4–10 and note the changes that spiritual life brings.

Ephesians 2:1–3 (Without Spiritual Life)	**Ephesians 2:4–10** (With Spiritual Life)
_____	_____
_____	_____
_____	_____

When you were dead in your sins and in the uncircumcision of your sinful nature, God made you alive with Christ. He forgave us all our sins, having canceled the written code, with its regulations, that was against us and that stood opposed to us; he took it away, nailing it to the cross. And having disarmed the powers and authorities, he made a public spectacle of them, triumphing over them by the cross. (Colossians 2:13–15)

How does Paul describe our spiritual condition when we were made alive by Christ? _____

_____

What did God do to change this? _____

_____

_____

How did it affect us? _____

_____

_____

Forgiveness is a precondition to spiritual life. Those who are spiritually dead are condemned by God's Law and enslaved by their own sinful nature. Christ's death wiped out the record of sin that made us God's enemies. This included the guilt of Adam's original sin that was credited to our account, along with all the interest we have compounded on that debt that by our own sin. In Colossians 2:14 the apostle Paul says that when God forgave us in Christ, He "cancelled out the certificate of debt consisting of decrees against us, which was hostile to us." Our debt was canceled when God "nailed it to the cross" by Christ's sacrifice.

You were taught, with regard to your former way of life, to put off your old self, which is being corrupted by its deceitful desires; to be made new in the attitude of your minds; and to put on the new self, created to be like God in true righteousness and holiness. (Ephesians 4:22–24)

In Ephesians 4:22 the apostle Paul refers to our "former way of life" and links it to our "old self." What does he say we are to do about it? _____

_____

_____

How is this possible? _____

_____

_____

How does the believer's "new self" differ from the "old self"? _____

_____

_____

Read Colossians 3:1–5. Then answer the following questions.

What is our position now that we are in Christ? _____

_____

_____

How should this affect the way we think? _____

_____

_____

How should our new position affect our behavior? _____

_____

_____

What specific areas does Paul say should change as a result of the new life we have received from Christ? _____

_____

_____

Read Colossians 3:6–10. Then answer the following questions.

Is change automatic in the Christian life? _____

_____

_____

What motivation does Paul provide for getting rid of those things that were a part of our former life? _____

_____

_____

Christ's death dealt with the penalty we were subject to because of sin. But the benefits of His work do not end there. Christ's resurrection dealt with the effects of sin. Christians have been "raised up" along with Christ, and their capacity to respond to God has been restored. This is the "new self" that believers are commanded to "put on."

MY RESPONSE

1. Do you see yourself as one who is spiritually dead or spiritually alive? _____

_____

_____

2. Compare Paul's list of attitudes and behaviors in Colossians 3:5–10. Which of these have been characteristic of you? _____

_____

_____

3. What concrete steps do you need to take to "put to death whatever belongs to your earthly nature" and to rid yourself of these things? _____

_____

_____

4. Why should you take such actions? _____

_____

_____

CONCLUSION

When we were separated from Christ, we were the objects of God's wrath. If it had not been for the intervention of His grace, we would have been separated for all eternity. Now that we have been seated in the heavenly realms in Christ, we face a radically different future. We have exchanged an eternity of hopelessness and regret for an endless future of God's boundless kindness. This has not been our own doing. It is the work of God. It was His purpose from the very beginning. We who were once the objects of wrath have become heavenly trophies of grace.

PRAYER

Give thanks for the transforming work of Christ. Ask God for the grace and power to rid yourself of the vestiges of the old self. Ask Him to help to follow through in your plans to "put them to death" by the power of the Cross.

THE MINISTRY
OF THE
HOLY SPIRIT

KEY PASSAGE: *And you also were included in Christ when you heard the word of truth, the gospel of your salvation. Having believed, you were marked in him with a seal, the promised Holy Spirit, who is a deposit guaranteeing our inheritance until the redemption of those who are God's possession—to the praise of his glory.* (Ephesians 1:13–14)

WISE WORDS

> *No one has understood the gospel who has not grasped that Christianity is first inward and spiritual, and secondly a divine work of grace.*
>
> JOHN R. W. STOTT

> *Christians are primarily the purchased redemption of God: God has purchased them to Himself by the precious blood of His Son. But, the purchase is one thing, and 'the delivery of the goods' another. . . . There remains, accordingly a 'day of redemption' yet in the future, unto which the purchased possession is to be brought. Meanwhile, because we are purchased and are God's possession, we are sealed to Him and to the fulfillment of the redemption, to take place on that day. And the seal is the Holy Spirit.*
>
> B. B. WARFIELD

THOUGHT STARTER

Why is the Holy Spirit the focus of so much controversy and discussion today? _____

_____

_____

How important is the ministry of the Spirit to the Christian life? _____

_____

_____

SCRIPTURE STUDY

One of the most important distinctives of Christian spirituality is the believer's unique relationship with the Holy Spirit. The Holy Spirit plays a central role both in our initial salvation experience and in the Christian life that follows conversion. The Christian life is a life in the Spirit.

Read John 3:1–8. Then answer the following questions.

What unasked question did Jesus answer for Nicodemus? _____

_____

_____

To what does Jesus compare the Holy Spirit? _____

_____

_____

What does this indicate about the Spirit's ministry? _____

_____

_____

What does the Holy Spirit do for us that we cannot do for ourselves? _____

_____

_____

Read John 16:5–11. Then answer the following questions.

Why did Jesus say that His departure was good for the disciples? _____

_____

_____

How does He refer to the Holy Spirit? _____

_____

_____

What does this title imply about the Spirit's ministry? _____

_____

_____

What does Jesus say that the Holy Spirit will do for the "world"? _____

_____

_____

The ministry of the Holy Spirit begins even before the believer's salvation experience. It is the Holy Spirit who convicts us of sin and convinces us of our need for Christ. When Jesus told the disciples that He would send the Holy Spirit, He promised that the Spirit would "convict the world of guilt in regard to sin and righteousness and judgment" (John 16:8). This is the language of the courtroom. To "convict" is to expose or bring to light. It is the Spirit's ministry to "the world," the work by which He makes sinners aware of their guilt, the nature of God's righteousness, and the inevitability of judgment.

Read Titus 3:3–7, and then answer the following questions.

How does Paul describe our pre-Christian experience in these verses? _____

_____

_____

What changed? _____

_____

_____

Why did God intervene? _____

_____

_____

What two aspects of the work of the Holy Spirit does Paul emphasize? _____

_____

_____

When we trust in Christ, the Holy Spirit imparts new life to us. Jesus referred to this as being "born again" (John 3:3, 8). The theological term for this work of the Holy Spirit is regeneration. When we are born again, we are cleansed of sin ("washed"; see Titus 3:5). Our guilt is taken away and we are given a new position as children of God. At the same time we are also given the capacity to live a new life ("renewal"; Titus 3:5).

Therefore, if anyone is in Christ, he is a new creation; the old has gone, the new has come! . . . Neither circumcision nor uncircumcision means anything; what counts is a new creation. (2 Corinthians 5:17; Galatians 6:15)

What do you think Paul means when he says that those who are in Christ are "a new creation"? _____

_____

_____

What evidence have you seen of this in your own life? _____

_____

_____

Now it is God who makes both us and you stand firm in Christ. He anointed us, set his seal of ownership on us, and put his Spirit in our hearts as a deposit, guaranteeing what is to come. (2 Corinthians 1:21–22)

Having believed, you were marked in [Christ] with a seal, the promised Holy Spirit, who is a deposit guaranteeing our inheritance until the redemption of those who are God's possession—to the praise of his glory. (Ephesians 1:13–14)

What two terms does Paul use to describe the Holy Spirit in these verses? _____

_____

_____

What does he say that the Holy Spirit does for us? _____

_____

_____

The presence of the Holy Spirit marks the believer as God's own child. Paul describes the Holy Spirit as a "seal." In the ancient world seals were often used to identify ownership and guarantee authenticity. We were sealed with the Holy Spirit when we believed, and His presence guarantees God's blessings to us until we receive the promised inheritance. He is also called a "deposit" or a "pledge." This term used in these two verses was used in other Greek writings to refer to the down payment or "earnest" paid on a piece of property. When Paul speaks of the Holy Spirit as the earnest that guarantees what is to come, he implies that part of the Holy Spirit's ministry is to give us a foretaste of what our final experience of salvation will be like.

Read Romans 5:1–5, and then answer these two questions:

How do we experience the love of God? _____

_____

_____

What must first be true of us before this can happen? _____

_____

_____

Read Romans 8:11–16, and then answer these two questions:

How does the Holy Spirit enable us to live godly lives? _____

_____

_____

Why does Paul refer to the Holy Spirit as "the Spirit of sonship"? _____

_____

_____

Read Romans 8:26–27, and then answer these two questions:

How does the Holy Spirit help our prayer life? _____

_____

_____

Why is this an encouragement? _____

_____

_____

Assurance of salvation is one of the ministries of the Holy Spirit. He "testifies with our spirit that we are God's children" (Romans 8:16). Doubts may still arise, but it is the Spirit that quiets them. The Holy Spirit is also called "the Spirit of sonship" or "the Spirit of adoption" in Romans 8:15. It is the Holy Spirit who prompts us to address God as a child would a father. He mediates our experience of God's love by "pouring" it into our hearts (Romans 5:5). He also exercises a ministry of prayer on our behalf. When we don't know how to pray for ourselves, we can be certain that the Holy Spirit is praying for us (Romans 8:26). Since His prayers reflect the mind of the Father and are always in accordance with His will, we can be certain that they will be answered favorably.

MY RESPONSE

1. Where have you experienced the ministry of the Holy Spirit recently? _____

_____

_____

2. How did it help you? _____

_____

_____

3. Where do you need His help most at this time? _____

_____

_____

4. How can He help you? _____

_____

_____

CONCLUSION

The Holy Spirit's ministry is a source of power for the Christian, but it is a mistake to think of Him as an impersonal force. He is a Person, not a power. Because He is a personal being, He spoke to the New Testament church and prays for us when we don't know how to pray (Luke 12:11–12; Acts 13:2; Romans 8:26). Because the Holy Spirit is a Person, He can be grieved by us (Ephesians 4:30). We grieve God's Spirit when we engage in unwholesome speech and when we allow bitterness and anger to divide the body of Christ (Ephesians 4:29, 31).

PRAYER

Give thanks for the ministry of the Holy Spirit in your life. Ask for the Spirit's help in the area identified above.

l e s s o n   f i v e

EVIDENCE
OF THE
SPIRIT

KEY PASSAGE: *But the fruit of the Spirit is love, joy, peace, patience, kindness, goodness, faithfulness, gentleness and self-control. Against such things there is no law.*
(Galatians 5:22–23)

WISE WORDS

The baptism by the Spirit does not necessarily mean a special endowment with power. It places us in a position in Christ that enables us to receive power, but the act of baptizing does not in itself guarantee that power will be experienced or displayed in the life.

CHARLES RYRIE

Although the sign gifts died in the first century, the Holy Spirit did not. We can affirm this theologically, but pragmatically we act as though the Holy Spirit died with the early church.

DANIEL B. WALLACE

THOUGHT STARTER

What do you think Wallace means when he says that *pragmatically we act as though the Holy Spirit died with the early church?* _____

_____

_____

What does he imply that we should not look for as evidence of the Spirit's ministry? _____

_____

_____

What kind of proof should we look for? _____

_____

_____

SCRIPTURE STUDY

Love never fails. But where there are prophecies, they will cease; where there are tongues, they will be stilled; where there is knowledge, it will pass away. For we know in part and we prophesy in part, but when perfection comes, the imperfect disappears. (1 Corinthians 13:8–10)

What does Paul say will happen to the spiritual gifts mentioned in these verses? _____

_____

_____

When will this happen? _____

_____

_____

When will "perfection" come? _____

_____

_____

Everyone was filled with awe, and many wonders and miraculous signs were done by the apostles. (Acts 2:43)

The things that mark an apostle—signs, wonders and miracles—were done among you with great perseverance. (2 Corinthians 12:12)

Who, according to these verses, exercised miraculous gifts during the New Testament era? _____

_____

_____

What does Paul imply when he refers to these as "things that mark an apostle"? _____

_____

_____

Consequently, you are no longer foreigners and aliens, but fellow citizens with God's people and members of God's household, built on the foundation of the apostles and prophets, with Christ Jesus himself as the chief cornerstone. (Ephesians 2:19–20)

How does Paul characterize the ministry of the apostles in Ephesians 2:20? _____

_____

_____

What does this imply about God's purpose for the sign gifts? _____

_____

_____

We have different gifts, according to the grace given us. If a man's gift is prophesying, let him use it in proportion to his faith. If it is serving, let him serve; if it is teaching, let him teach; if it is encouraging, let him encourage; if it is contributing to the needs of others, let him give generously; if it is leadership, let him govern diligently; if it is showing mercy, let him do it cheerfully. (Romans 12:6–8)

Is it wrong to want to have spiritual gifts? _____

_____

_____

Should all believers expect to have the same gifts? _____

_____

_____

There are different kinds of gifts, but the same Spirit. There are different kinds of service, but the same Lord. There are different kinds of working, but the same God works all of them in all men. Now to each one the manifestation of the Spirit is given for the common good. To one there is given through the Spirit the message of wisdom, to another the message of knowledge by means of the same Spirit, to another faith by the same Spirit, to another gifts of healing by that one Spirit, to another miraculous powers, to another prophecy, to another distinguishing between spirits, to another speaking in different kinds of tongues, and to still another the interpretation of tongues. All these are the work of one and the same Spirit, and he gives them to each one, just as he determines. (1 Corinthians 12:4–11)

This salvation, which was first announced by the Lord, was confirmed to us by those who heard him. God also testified to it by signs, wonders and various miracles, and gifts of the Holy Spirit distributed according to his will. (Hebrews 2:3–4)

Who determines what spiritual gifts a believer receives? _____

_____

_____

What is the basis for granting a certain gift to one believer and a different gift to another? _____

_____

_____

What should our motive be when exercising a spiritual gift? _____

_____

_____

The Holy Spirit is not at our beck and call. He distributes gifts throughout the body of Christ according to His sovereign will. Every believer is given the Holy Spirit and is gifted in some way, but not everyone has the same gifts (1 Corinthians 12:29–30). We are told to desire the greater gifts, but are also reminded that we cannot control which ones will be given to us. "All these are the work of one and the same Spirit," the apostle Paul declares, "and he gives them to each one, just as he determines" (1 Corinthians 12:11).

Read Galatians 5:16–26. Then answer the following questions.

What is the difference between the "gifts" of the Spirit and the "fruit" of the Spirit? _____

_____

_____

Which does Paul emphasize when he tells us to "live by the Spirit" and "to keep in step with the Spirit"? _____

_____

_____

Do we have any personal responsibility when it comes to producing the fruit of the Spirit? _____

_____

_____

MY RESPONSE

Review your actions over the past five days. Where did you see evidence of the fruit of the Spirit in your life? Where was the fruit of the Spirit needed but lacking? Be specific.

Fruit	In Evidence	Needed
Love:		
Joy:		
Peace:		
Patience:		
Kindness:		
Goodness:		
Faithfulness:		
Gentleness:		
Self-Control:		

CONCLUSION

Ironically, the church's ongoing dispute over spiritual gifts has obscured what really should be regarded as the primary evidence for the presence of the Holy Spirit in the believer's life. The Holy Spirit's presence is most often seen, not in gifts of the Spirit but in the fruit of the Spirit (Galatians 5:22–23). Qualities like love, joy, peace, patience, kindness, goodness, faithfulness, gentleness, and self-control are the everyday miracles that prove to the world that Christ has done a transforming work in the believer's life. They are the marks of true spirituality among believers. Spiritual gifts are important to the life of the church but they do not guarantee spiritual maturity.

PRAYER

Ask God for an opportunity to demonstrate the fruit of the Spirit today. Pray for the areas of need identified above.

OBSTACLES TO
DISCIPLESHIP

THE GROWTH PROCESS

KEY PASSAGE: *Anyone who lives on milk, being still an infant, is not acquainted with the teaching about righteousness. But solid food is for the mature, who by constant use have trained themselves to distinguish good from evil.*
(Hebrews 5:13–14)

WISE WORDS

You know it is always regarded a great event in the family when a child can feed himself. . . . At first perhaps he uses the spoon upside down. But by and by he handles it all right, and mother, or perhaps sister, claps her hands and says, "Just see, baby's feeding himself!" Well, what we need as Christians is to be able to feed ourselves. How many there are who sit helpless and listless, with open mouths, hungry for spiritual things, and the minister has to try to feed them, while the Bible is a feast prepared into which they never venture.
D. L. MOODY

Were our affections filled, taken up, and possessed with these things, as it is our duty that they should be . . . what access could sin, with its painted pleasures, with its sugared poisons . . . have to our souls?
JOHN OWEN

THOUGHT STARTER

Why do you think some Christians fail to grow? _____

_____

_____

What is necessary in order for Christians to grow? _____

_____

_____

Are you satisfied with your own rate of spiritual growth? Why or why not? _____

_____

_____

SCRIPTURE STUDY

In the natural realm, growth is normal. We expect infants to grow and become children, children to develop into adolescents, and adolescents to grow into adulthood. The same is true in the spiritual realm.

Normally, spiritual birth should lead to spiritual growth and development. Sadly, this is not always the case. Some who have professed faith in Jesus Christ appear to suffer from "stunted" growth. Years after their conversion they are still much the same as when they first believed. The author of the book of Hebrews describes this problem in the following passage.

In fact, though by this time you ought to be teachers, you need someone to teach you the elementary truths of God's word all over again. You need milk, not solid food! Anyone who lives on milk, being still an infant, is not acquainted with the teaching about righteousness. But solid food is for the mature, who by constant use have trained themselves to distinguish good from evil. (Hebrews 5:12–14)

What did the author of the book of Hebrews say was the problem with his readers? _____
_____
_____

What should have been true of them instead? _____
_____
_____

To what is he referring when he speaks of "milk"? What is "solid food"? _____
_____
_____

How does he describe those who are in a state of spiritual infancy? _____
_____
_____

The author of Hebrews complained that at the time when his readers ought to have been able to teach others they needed to be taught the "elementary truths of God's word" all over again (Hebrews 5:12). One of the assumptions behind his complaint is the expectation that normal Christian growth should occur over time. It also implies that growth is progressive. It is not attained instantaneously when we experience the new birth.

Open your Bible to Hebrews 6 to read about this progressive growth. First read Hebrews 6:1–3 and answer the following questions.

What does the writer of Hebrews urge his readers to do? _____
_____
_____

What do you think he means when he urges them to "leave behind" the elementary teachings about Christ? _____
_____
_____

Next read Hebrews 6:4–9; Then answer the following questions.

Why should we be concerned if we show no evidence of spiritual maturity? _____

_____

_____

To what does the author compare those who fail to produce spiritual fruit in their lives? _____

_____

_____

What does he expect will be true of his readers? _____

_____

_____

We do not earn God's love and acceptance by growing spiritually. Like salvation, spiritual growth is a result of God's gracious work in our lives. If this is so, however, the absence of spiritual growth may indicate that those who remain in a state of spiritual immaturity were never truly Christ's to begin with. The author of the book of Hebrews warned his readers not to be complacent about their spiritual life.

MY RESPONSE

In the space below, draw a timeline of your own spiritual development. Note major spiritual milestones.

What have been the most important factors that have contributed to your spiritual development? _____

_____

_____

Should you be satisfied with your current level of spiritual growth? Why or why not? _____

_____

_____

Where do you need to grow most? _____

_____

_____

CONCLUSION

Like any parent, God is pleased when His children show evidence of growth in their lives. Those who know Christ do not become spiritually mature the instant they believe but go through a process of spiritual development. When we see evidence of spiritual growth, we should feel a mixture of joy and holy discontent—joy because we know that growth is evidence of the reality of God's grace in our lives, and discontent because we are eager to go on to deeper levels of maturity.

PRAYER

Review the past week. Give thanks for each evidence of spiritual growth that you see.

STAGES OF GROWTH

KEY PASSAGE: *I write to you, fathers, because you have known him who is from the beginning. I write to you, young men, because you have overcome the evil one. I write to you, dear children, because you have known the Father. I write to you, fathers, because you have known him who is from the beginning. I write to you, young men, because you are strong, and the word of God lives in you, and you have overcome the evil one.*
(1 John 2:13–14)

WISE WORDS

There are four stages of growth in Christian maturity: Love of self for self's sake. Love of God for self's sake. Love of God for God's sake. Love of self for God's sake.
BERNARD OF CLAIRVAUX

I don't think God is interested in our success. He is interested in our maturity.
FRED SMITH (FOUNDER OF UNITED PARCEL SERVICE)

THOUGHT STARTER

How many stages can you identify in your own spiritual growth and development? _____
_____
_____

What are the chief characteristics of each stage? _____
_____
_____

How does one move from one stage to another? _____
_____
_____

SCRIPTURE STUDY

Spiritual growth, like human growth, develops in stages. John mentions three stages in 1 John 2:13–14, our key passage. We could label these stages spiritual infancy, adolescence, and maturity.

What parallels between physical and spiritual growth do you think John saw that prompted him to identify in verses 13–14 these three stages?

	Physical Growth	**Spiritual Growth**
Infancy:		
Adolescence:		
Maturity:		

What do spiritual infancy and spiritual maturity both have in common, according to verses 13–14? _____

_____

_____

What is the difference between the knowledge of the Father at each of these stages? _____

_____

_____

Now this is eternal life: that they may know you, the only true God, and Jesus Christ, whom you have sent. (John 17:3)

Why does Jesus equate knowing God through Jesus Christ with eternal life? _____

_____

_____

In the past God spoke to our forefathers through the prophets at many times and in various ways, but in these last days he has spoken to us by his Son, whom he appointed heir of all things, and through whom he made the universe. The Son is the radiance of God's glory and the exact representation of his being, sustaining all things by his powerful word. After he had provided purification for sins, he sat down at the right hand of the Majesty in heaven. (Hebrews 1:1–3)

How does Jesus Christ make it possible for us to know the Father? _____

_____

_____

What is His relationship to the Father, according to Hebrews 1:1–3? _____

_____

_____

What does the author of Hebrews say that Christ has done that has made it possible for us to know the Father?

_____

_____

_____

Do we ever outgrow our need to know God in this sense? Why or why not? _____

_____

_____

Read John 14:1–11, and then answer the following questions.

What prompted Philip to ask, "Show us the way to the Father"? _____

_____

_____

Do you think it was a reasonable question, in view of the circumstances? _____

_____

_____

How did Jesus respond to his question? _____

_____

_____

What does Jesus imply should have been true of the disciples at this point? _____

_____

_____

Knowing God is both the beginning and end of the Christian life. This knowledge is not primarily a cognitive awareness of biblical doctrine but a growing relationship. It begins with the knowledge of what God the Father has done for us through the person of Jesus Christ. Jesus reveals the Father and gives us access to a relationship with Him when we place our trust in Him. This relationship is deepened as our knowledge and experience of God grow. The spiritual infant knows God by faith. The spiritually mature believer knows Him by faith and experience.

Read the following verses and identify the type of growth that is mentioned in each.

1 Corinthians 3:6 _____

_____

2 Corinthians 10:15 _____

_____

Ephesians 4:15–16 _____

_____

Colossians 1:10 _____

_____

Colossians 2:18–19 _____

_____

2 Thessalonians 1:3 _____

_____

1 Peter 2:2 _____

_____

2 Peter 3:18 _____

_____

Read Romans 7:15–25. Then answer the following questions.

How does Paul describe his struggle with sin in these verses? _____

_____

_____

At what stage in his personal spiritual development do you think this struggle took place? _____

_____

_____

If the mark of spiritual infancy is a foundational knowledge of the Father through faith in Christ, the mark of spiritual adolescence is the progressive victory over temptation. Spiritual maturity is characterized by a settled knowledge of the Father—a knowledge that is grounded both in faith and experience. We can conclude from this that normal spiritual development is characterized by growth in obedience as well as growth in knowledge. The believer's skill in saying no to sin and yes to God increases as he or she progresses in the Christian life. This does not necessarily mean that our struggle with the flesh diminishes as we mature. In some cases it may even grow more intense. This is because understanding of sin deepens as we mature to the point where it not only includes our actions but also the motives that prompt them.

We who are strong ought to bear with the failings of the weak and not to please ourselves. (Romans 15:1)

And we urge you, brothers, warn those who are idle, encourage the timid, help the weak, be patient with everyone. (1 Thessalonians 5:14)

Should we expect everyone to be at the same level spiritually? _____

_____

_____

How should we treat those who are less mature? _____

_____

_____

MY RESPONSE

1. In what area of your spiritual life would you most like to see growth in the next six months? _____

_____

_____

2. What would that growth look like? _____

_____

_____

3. What steps do you need to take to insure that such growth occurs? _____

_____

_____

4. What do you need to do today to begin the process of growth? _____

_____

_____

CONCLUSION

Not every Christian is in the same place spiritually. Spiritual growth is progressive. If it moves from infancy to adulthood, we shouldn't be too surprised to find a range of spiritual levels in the church. The church's strategy for discipleship must take this into account by providing a range of opportunities for believers at every level of development. This is also good to know if you are at an early stage in your spiritual development. In time you will grow. It is very likely that you have already grown more than you realize.

PRAYER

Thank God for the spiritual growth you have seen. Ask Him to help you grow further in the area you identified above.

STUNTED
GROWTH

KEY PASSAGE: *Brothers, I could not address you as spiritual but as worldly—mere infants in Christ. I gave you milk, not solid food, for you were not yet ready for it. Indeed, you are still not ready. You are still worldly. For since there is jealousy and quarreling among you, are you not worldly? Are you not acting like mere men?* (1 Corinthians 3:1–3)

WISE WORDS

So we justly pay the penalty of our laziness in that most of us spend our lives in the elementary stages like children.

JOHN CALVIN

Milk, as the appropriate food of babes and sickly persons, is a fit emblem of elementary instruction, suited to imbecile minds and limited acquirements.

JOHN BROWN

THOUGHT STARTER

Think of someone who seems to be "stuck" in his or her spiritual development? What is the evidence that his or her spiritual growth has been "stunted"? _____

_____

_____

Why do you think this person is not as mature as he or she should be? _____

_____

_____

Is there anything the person can do to change this? If so, what? _____

_____

_____

SCRIPTURE STUDY

Everyone who trusts in Christ has the potential to grow spiritually, but some believers seem to suffer from "stunted" growth. Paul described these kind of believers as "fleshly," or "worldly," and complained that they were unable to accept "solid food." They had remained as spiritual infants.

The man without the Spirit does not accept the things that come from the Spirit of God, for they are foolishness to him, and he cannot understand them, because they are spiritually discerned. (1 Corinthians 2:14)

*The "man without the Spirit" is an unbeliever (compare Romans 8:9). How does such a person respond to spiritual truth?*_____

_____

_____

*Why does this person respond in this manner?*_____

_____

_____

Brothers, I could not address you as spiritual but as worldly—mere infants in Christ. I gave you milk, not solid food, for you were not yet ready for it. Indeed, you are still not ready. You are still worldly. (1 Corinthians 3:1–3)

*What do you think Paul meant when he described these Christians as "worldly"?*_____

_____

_____

*What was the evidence of this worldliness?*_____

_____

_____

*Is this what we usually mean when we describe someone as "worldly"?*_____

_____

_____

*How did their spiritual condition affect the way Paul ministered to them?*_____

_____

_____

You are still worldly. For since there is jealousy and quarreling among you, are you not worldly? Are you not acting like mere men? For when one says, "I follow Paul," and another, "I follow Apollos," are you not mere men? What, after all, is Apollos? And what is Paul? Only servants, through whom you came to believe—as the Lord has assigned to each his task. (1 Corinthians 3:3–5)

*What was the evidence of Corinthian worldliness?*_____

_____

_____

What do the "man without the Spirit" and the "worldly" believer have in common? _____
_____
_____

What is different about them? _____
_____
_____

We are fools for Christ, but you are so wise in Christ! We are weak, but you are strong! You are honored, we are dishonored! (1 Corinthians 4:10)

Using sarcasm, the apostle Paul reveals the attitude many in the Corinthian church had about themselves. How did the Corinthians view themselves? _____
_____
_____

Why do you think they regarded themselves in this way? _____
_____
_____

There is an important but subtle difference between the unbeliever and the worldly Christian. The unbeliever does not possess the Holy Spirit. In 1 Corinthians 2:14 the unbeliever is literally characterized as "soulish." Such a person cannot accept the things that come from God's Spirit (i.e., the truths Paul teaches) because they are "spiritually discerned." The unbeliever lacks the spiritual capacity to be responsive to God's truth and cannot see its value. The same cannot be said of the "spiritual infant" described in 1 Corinthians 3:1. This person is "spiritual" in the sense that he possesses the Holy Spirit, but he is not spiritually mature. The spiritual infant is "worldly" or "fleshly." This condition forced Paul to adjust his teaching to suit the Corinthians' spiritual state. He treated them like spiritual babies and gave them "milk" instead of "solid food" (1 Corinthians 3:2).

MY RESPONSE

1. Rewrite 1 Corinthians 2:14–3:5 as if Paul were writing to your church today. What examples would he use to describe "worldliness"? _____
_____
_____

2. Imagine that you are creating a ruler that will measure spiritual growth. How will you measure development? What will you use for increments? _____
_____
_____

CONCLUSION

It is sobering to consider that the Corinthians probably did not see themselves as Paul did. They considered themselves to be spiritual and mature when in reality they were fleshly and immature. The proof of their immaturity was the presence of jealousy and quarreling within the church. We tend to think of spiritual maturity in terms of what a person knows. If someone discusses difficult doctrines, reads complex theological works, or listens to the most capable Bible teachers, then we say that he is mature. Paul's rebuke indicates that God uses a different standard to measure spiritual maturity. The mark of spiritual maturity is not merely the possession of knowledge. True maturity is characterized by applied knowledge. Jesus Himself emphasized this when He said: "If you hold to my teaching, you are really my disciples" (John 8:31).

PRAYER

Pray for someone you know who is spiritually immature. Ask God to help him or her to become mature. Pray for any areas of immaturity that you may have identified in your own life.

GROWTH AND EFFORT

KEY PASSAGE: *For this very reason, make every effort to add to your faith goodness; and to goodness, knowledge; and to knowledge, self-control; and to self-control, perseverance; and to perseverance, godliness; and to godliness, brotherly kindness; and to brotherly kindness, love.*
(2 Peter 1:5–7)

WISE WORDS

Our bodies are shaped into a specific character and laden with specific skills and tendencies by our experiences, including those we voluntarily undertake. There is some latitude within which our character is formed by ourselves. Through the instrumentality of his life-giving word, God in regeneration renews our original capacity for divine interaction. But our body's substance is only to be transformed totally by actions and events in which we choose to participate from day to day.
DALLAS WILLARD

Because by and large we do not expect people to experience ongoing transformation, we are not led to question whether perhaps the standard prescriptions for spiritual growth being given in the church are truly adequate to lead people into a transformed way of life.
JOHN ORTBERG

THOUGHT STARTER

Is making an effort in the spiritual life inconsistent with the Bible's theology of grace? Why or why not? _____

_____

_____

How would you distinguish legitimate spiritual effort from legalism? _____

_____

_____

What would be an example of legitimate spiritual effort? _____

_____

_____

What would be an example of legalism? _____

_____

_____

SCRIPTURE STUDY

Although spiritual growth is ultimately a matter of grace, it requires a measure of Spirit empowered effort to take place. We do not become spiritually mature simply because we acquire doctrinal and biblical knowledge. Truth is a necessary catalyst for spiritual growth but genuine spiritual growth occurs only when truth is applied. At every stage in our development we are responsible to add to the knowledge and virtues that we have already attained in Christ.

Grace and peace be yours in abundance through the knowledge of God and of Jesus our Lord. His divine power has given us everything we need for life and godliness through our knowledge of him who called us by his own glory and goodness. Through these he has given us his very great and precious promises, so that through them you may participate in the divine nature and escape the corruption in the world caused by evil desires. For this very reason, make every effort to add to your faith goodness; and to goodness, knowledge; and to knowledge, self-control; and to self-control, perseverance; and to perseverance, godliness; and to godliness, brotherly kindness; and to brotherly kindness, love. (2 Peter 1:2–7)

How has God made provision for the believer's spiritual growth? _____

_____

_____

If we are to grow spiritually, what does Peter say must be true of us first? _____

_____

_____

In what areas does Peter say that we see growth after we have trusted in Christ? _____

_____

_____

Spiritual growth is the result of God's power. His power has provided all that we need for a life of godliness. We access God's power by responding to the promises He has given in His Word. However, as great as God's power and promises are, they do not guarantee growth. We also have a responsibility to "make every effort" to grow spiritually.

Do you not know that in a race all the runners run, but only one gets the prize? Run in such a way as to get the prize. Everyone who competes in the games goes into strict training. They do it to get a crown that will not last; but we do it to get a crown that will last forever. Therefore I do not run like a man running aimlessly; I do not fight like a man beating the air. No, I beat my body and make it my slave so that after I have preached to others, I myself will not be disqualified for the prize. (1 Corinthians 9:24–27)

How does Paul describe his approach to his own spiritual life and ministry? _____

_____

_____

GROWTH AND EFFORT 115

What kind of effort did this require of him? _____

_____

_____

Why did Paul feel that this kind of divinely enabled effort was necessary? _____

_____

_____

Read Ephesians 4:11–13. Then answer the following questions.

In what sense is spiritual growth a "group" activity as well as an individual effort? _____

_____

_____

What marks of corporate maturity does Paul describe in these verses? _____

_____

_____

What role do gifted individuals within the body of Christ play in this growth process? _____

_____

_____

What is the ultimate purpose of their ministry? _____

_____

_____

Then we will no longer be infants, tossed back and forth by the waves, and blown here and there by every wind of teaching and by the cunning and craftiness of men in their deceitful scheming. Instead, speaking the truth in love, we will in all things grow up into him who is the Head, that is, Christ. From him the whole body, joined and held together by every supporting ligament, grows and builds itself up in love, as each part does its work. (Ephesians 4:14–16)

How does Paul say the body of Christ grows? _____

_____

_____

What does "speaking the truth in love" have to do with the gifts Paul identifies in the previous verses? _____

_____

_____

Who is the standard against which our spiritual maturity should be measured? _____

_____

_____

MY RESPONSE

1. Paul compared himself to a runner and a boxer when describing the effort required of him in living the Christian life. What kind of athlete would best describe your approach to the Christian life? Why? _____

_____

_____

2. If you were to rate the amount of effort you are currently investing in your own spiritual growth, where would you place yourself on the scale below?

No Effort		Some Effort		Every Effort
1	2	3	4	5

3. How would you rate yourself if you were to rate the amount of effort you are currently investing in helping others to grow spiritually?

No Effort		Some Effort		Every Effort
1	2	3	4	5

4. Are you satisfied with how you have rated yourself above? If not, what should you do to change? _____

_____

_____

CONCLUSION

The Scriptures repeatedly link spiritual maturity with grace, knowledge, and effort. Spiritual growth is a work of God's grace and cannot be achieved solely by human effort. Yet it is also a result of both individual and corporate activity. The individual believer strives to grow in grace and is built up by the ministry of others in the body of Christ. The believer's effort is grounded in the truth of God's Word and involves both understanding biblical truth and acting upon it.

PRAYER

Choose an area where you feel that more effort is needed in your Christian life. Think about one concrete step you can take to "make every effort" to grow in grace in this area. Ask God to help you follow through.

INGREDIENTS
FOR GROWTH

KEY PASSAGE: *Like newborn babies, crave pure spiritual milk, so that by it you may grow up in your salvation, now that you have tasted that the Lord is good.*
(1 Peter 2:2–3)

WISE WORDS

There are means which God has appointed to help man in his endeavours to approach Him. . . . Public worship, reading the Bible, hearing the Gospel preached—these are the kinds of things to which I refer. Doubtless no one can change his own heart, or wipe away one of his sins, or make himself in the least degree acceptable to God; but I do say that if man could do nothing but sit still, Christ would never have said "Strive."

J. C. RYLE

We are in a growing-learning relationship, always. A disciple is a learner, but not in the academic setting of a schoolroom, rather at the work site of a craftsman. We do not acquire information about God but skills in faith.

EUGENE PETERSON

THOUGHT STARTER

Some of the tools God uses to foster the believer's spiritual development are obvious, such as Bible study, prayer, and corporate worship. Can you think of any other means that God uses to help you grow spiritually? _____

_____

_____

What conditions must be met in order for spiritual growth to take place in your life? _____

_____

_____

SCRIPTURE STUDY

When it comes to spiritual growth, we must avoid two opposite but equally dangerous extremes. One extreme is to exalt the means used by God to foster spiritual growth beyond measure. This leads to spiritual pride and legalism. The other extreme is to ignore the means that God has provided for spiritual growth. This view confuses dependency upon divine grace with spiritual sloth. Growth is entirely a matter of grace, but it is grace that is experienced in connection with certain practices.

You diligently study the Scriptures because you think that by them you possess eternal life. These are the Scriptures that testify about me, yet you refuse to come to me to have life. (John 5:39–40)

Those Jesus criticizes in these verses were serious students of God's Word. Why didn't they benefit from their effort? _____

_____

_____

What did they need to do first? _____

_____

_____

And when you pray, do not be like the hypocrites, for they love to pray standing in the synagogues and on the street corners to be seen by men. I tell you the truth, they have received their reward in full. But when you pray, go into your room, close the door and pray to your Father, who is unseen. Then your Father, who sees what is done in secret, will reward you. And when you pray, do not keep on babbling like pagans, for they think they will be heard because of their many words. Do not be like them, for your Father knows what you need before you ask him. (Matthew 6:5–8)

Which two groups does Jesus criticize in these verses? _____

_____

_____

How does each group approach prayer? _____

_____

_____

What is wrong with these approaches? _____

_____

_____

If Jesus were saying this today, what kind of specific examples might He give? _____

_____

_____

You are still worldly. For since there is jealousy and quarreling among you, are you not worldly? Are you not acting like mere men? For when one says, "I follow Paul," and another, "I follow Apollos," are you not mere men? What, after all, is Apollos? And what is Paul? Only servants, through whom you came to believe—as the Lord has assigned to each his task. I planted the seed, Apollos watered it, but God made it grow. (1 Corinthians 3:3–6)

How did the Corinthians view those God had used to teach them? _____

_____

_____

Was it a mistake for them to expect God to use human teachers to help them grow spiritually? _____

_____

_____

Where did they go wrong? _____

_____

_____

God could have chosen to bring people to new life in Christ without human instrumentality, but instead He entrusted the gospel to the church and commanded that it be preached throughout the whole world (Matthew 24:14; 28:18–20). He could also have made it so that the new believer would instantaneously grow from spiritual infancy to maturity in a moment. Instead, He ordained that spiritual development take place over time and be linked to certain means that foster growth.

Therefore, rid yourselves of all malice and all deceit, hypocrisy, envy, and slander of every kind. Like newborn babies, crave pure spiritual milk, so that by it you may grow up in your salvation, now that you have tasted that the Lord is good. (1 Peter 2:1–3)

How are we to view God's Word? _____

_____

_____

Is there anything that we can do to "crave" God's Word? _____

_____

_____

What else does Peter say that we are to do in conjunction with our study of the Scriptures? _____

_____

_____

Peter does not compare God's Word to an "acquired" taste like vegetables, but to milk, something that infants naturally crave. He also links this longing to personal experience. How do we develop the craving for a particular food in the natural realm? We taste it and find that we like it. This same principle operates in the spiritual realm. The best way to develop a hunger for God's Word is to "taste that the Lord is good."

For this reason, since the day we heard about you, we have not stopped praying for you and asking God to fill you with the knowledge of his will through all spiritual wisdom and understanding. And we pray this in order that you may live a life worthy of the Lord and may please him in every way: bearing fruit in every good work, growing in the knowledge of God, being strengthened with all power according to his glorious might so that you may have great endurance and patience, and joyfully giving thanks to the Father, who has qualified you to share in the inheritance of the saints in the kingdom of light. (Colossians 1:9–12)

What did Paul expect God to do for the Colossian believers as a result of his prayer? _____

_____

_____

What did he expect the Colossians to do for themselves as a result of his prayer? _____

_____

_____

Open my eyes that I may see wonderful things in your law. (Psalm 119:18)

If any of you lacks wisdom, he should ask God, who gives generously to all without finding fault, and it will be given to him. But when he asks, he must believe and not doubt, because he who doubts is like a wave of the sea, blown and tossed by the wind. That man should not think he will receive anything from the Lord; he is a double-minded man, unstable in all he does. (James 1:5–8)

What do these verses imply about the relationship between prayer and Bible study? _____

_____

_____

James says that prayer must be accompanied by genuine faith. How does this kind of prayer differ from the type of prayer Jesus condemns in Matthew 6:7–8? _____

_____

_____

MY RESPONSE

1. How is God currently using each of the following to help you become more like Christ?

Bible Study: _____

_____

Prayer: _____

_____

Church: _____

_____

Trials: _____

_____

Friendships: _____

_____

Enemies: _____

_____

Work: _____

_____

2. What else is God using to foster your spiritual growth? _____

_____

_____

CONCLUSION

God is the ultimate source of all spiritual development, but He has chosen to use specific means to promote it. Chief among them are prayer and the Scriptures. Those who neglect the appointed means of growth and fail to practice Christian virtues will see their spiritual lives decline. Graces previously acquired may disappear. They may even begin to question whether there was ever a genuine transformation in their lives in the first place. When they ought to be mature enough to teach others, they will need to go back to kindergarten and learn the first principles of the Christian life all over again.

PRAYER

Using Colossians 1:9–12 as a pattern, pray for the spiritual growth of someone you know.

THE
MACHINERY OF
HOLINESS

FALLEN
TEMPLES

KEY PASSAGE: *For in my inner being I delight in God's law; but I see another law at work in the members of my body, waging war against the law of my mind and making me a prisoner of the law of sin at work within my members.*
(Romans 7:22–23)

WISE WORDS

Now when Paul urges believers to cleanse themselves of every defilement of flesh and spirit, he points out the two parts in which the filth of sin resides.

JOHN CALVIN

More spiritual failure is due, I believe, to this cause than to any other: the failure to recognize this living body as having anything to do with worship or holy sacrifice. This body is, quite simply, the starting place. Failure here is failure everywhere else.

ELISABETH ELLIOT

THOUGHT STARTER

Why is the body important to the spiritual life? _____

_____

_____

Does the body affect the spirit? If so, how? _____

_____

_____

How does the spirit affect the body? _____

_____

_____

What would you say to someone who argued that since God is a spirit, it does not matter what we do with our bodies? _____

_____

_____

SCRIPTURE STUDY

The LORD God formed the man from the dust of the ground and breathed into his nostrils the breath of life, and the man became a living being. (Genesis 2:7)

What two distinct components make up man's nature? _____

_____

_____

How did the human body originate? _____

_____

_____

Man was created to be both a material and an immaterial being. He was formed out of the dust of the earth and given the "breath of life" by God. Men and women are both physical and spiritual in nature. The two are distinct from one another but there is an important relationship between them. The spirit gives life to the body and the actions of the body express the intent of the spirit. Both were the creation of God.

Then Abraham spoke up again: "Now that I have been so bold as to speak to the LORD, though I am nothing but dust and ashes." (Genesis 18:27)

As a father has compassion on his children, so the LORD has compassion on those who fear him; for he knows how we are formed, he remembers that we are dust. (Psalm 103:13–14)

Does the fact that man was formed from the dust of the ground suggest anything about the body? If so, what?

_____

_____

_____

To Adam he said, "Because you listened to your wife and ate from the tree about which I commanded you, 'You must not eat of it,' Cursed is the ground because of you; through painful toil you will eat of it all the days of your life. It will produce thorns and thistles for you, and you will eat the plants of the field. By the sweat of your brow you will eat your food until you return to the ground, since from it you were taken; for dust you are and to dust you will return." (Genesis 3:17–19)

List the consequences of Adam's disobedience that are described in these verses.

What physical consequence did sin have for Adam? _____

_____

_____

Read 1 Corinthians 15:41–49, and then answer the following question.

In the above passage, Paul compares Adam ("the first Adam") with Christ ("the last Adam"). How do they differ from one another?

First Adam	**Last Adam**
_____	_____
_____	_____
_____	_____

The body is perishable by nature and must be made imperishable before it can enjoy the benefits of the kingdom. However, the problem of flesh is more than a matter of mere physical weakness and decay. Ultimately, our fleshly desires are a matter of rebellion. Adam's single act of disobedience made a permanent imprint on all his descendants. This stamp of sin skewed their thoughts and actions in the direction of disobedience.

Read Romans 7:14–25 and summarize Paul's complaint in your own words.

What other law did Paul find at work each time he tried to obey God's Law? _____

_____

_____

Where did he see this Law operating? _____

_____

_____

Next read Romans 8:1–4 and then answer the following questions.

What provision has God made for dealing with the struggle Paul describes in Romans 7:14–25? _____

_____

_____

How should this affect the way you respond to the sinful nature? _____

_____

_____

MY RESPONSE

1. Can you think of a recent occasion when you became aware of the struggle between your good intentions and the sinful nature? _____

_____

_____

2. Describe how you felt at the time. _____

_____

_____

3. Did you turn to Christ to help you say no to the sinful nature? _____

_____

_____

4. What do you plan to do the next time you feel the tug of the sinful nature? _____

_____

_____

CONCLUSION

Good intentions, determination, or sheer human willpower are not enough to overcome the sinful nature. It exerts a powerful influence on the members of our body. Only Christ's death and resurrection are strong enough to counter its effect. It is the presence of the sinful nature—the internal sin principle present in every descendant of Adam—that has perverted what was meant to be a holy vessel into a "body of death."

PRAYER

Using Paul's inspired words in Romans 7:25–8:4 as the basis for your prayer, give thanks to God for His provision for dealing with the sinful nature.

JESUS
AND THE
BODY

KEY PASSAGE: *Once you were alienated from God and were enemies in your minds because of your evil behavior. But now he has reconciled you by Christ's physical body through death to present you holy in his sight, without blemish and free from accusation.*
(Colossians 1:21–22)

WISE WORDS

The fact is that Jesus Christ was veiled in the flesh rather than revealed in the flesh. The flesh was the form which God took for manifestation; but the flesh actually became an obscuring medium. It was his humanity that impressed men, and not his divinity. Even his disciples who walked with him closely for three years, seem to have had doubts of his divinity to the very last, because that which impressed them most, and which was most apparent, was his humanity, and not the divine nature which dwelt in him.
ARTHUR TAPPAN PIERSON

Veiled in flesh the Godhead see,
Hail the incarnate Deity,
Pleased as man with men to dwell,
Jesus, our Emmanuel.

CHARLES WESLEY

THOUGHT STARTER

Which do you think people find harder to accept today, Christ's humanity or His divinity? Why? _____

_____

_____

In what ways is the humanity of Christ a source of encouragement to the believer? _____

_____

_____

SCRIPTURE STUDY

The greatest evidence for both the dignity and the spiritual significance of the physical body is found in the Incarnation. At the Incarnation, Jesus Christ, who already existed as God, took to himself a human nature. One aspect of that nature was a physical body.

The birth of Christ involved both natural and supernatural events. Read Matthew 1:18–25 and Luke 2:1–7 and identify those aspects of Christ's birth that fit each.

Natural	Supernatural
_____	_____
_____	_____
_____	_____

Jesus' body was a real human body and not a phantasm. It had all the natural attributes common to us, apart from sin. Although it was miraculously conceived in Mary's womb, it was delivered after the normal period of fetal development (Luke 2:6–7). It grew in size and increased in ability. The fact that Jesus grew in wisdom as well as in stature (v. 52) implies that His growth in knowledge and understanding correlated with His physical development. Like other human infants Jesus had to learn to walk and talk. His human thought processes developed from simple to more complex.

What do the following passages indicate about Christ's human nature?

John 1:14 _____

_____

_____

John 4:5–6 _____

_____

_____

John 11:5–21 _____

_____

_____

John 19:32–34 _____

_____

_____

1 John 1:1 _____

_____

_____

Jesus' body was also subject to ordinary human weaknesses. When it was deprived of food, He became hungry. When it was subjected to physical exertion, He grew weary. Like the rest of us, Jesus slept when He was tired and drank when He was thirsty. It was a body that could be seen and touched and could only be in one place at a time.

Read Matthew 4:1–11. To what aspects of Christ's human nature did Satan appeal during Jesus' temptation in the wilderness?

Verses 1–3: _____

_____

_____

Verses 4–7: _____

_____

_____

Verses 8–11: _____

_____

_____

What does this encounter teach us about His human nature? _____

_____

_____

Satan "took" Jesus and "had Him stand" on the highest point of the temple in Jerusalem. Then he challenged Jesus to throw Himself down, citing the promise of Psalm 91:12 that the angels would lift Him up in their hands to keep Him from being dashed on the stones. This implies that Jesus' body was subject to the law of gravity. Yet because He was God as well as man, Jesus could also choose to act in accordance with His divine nature. Consequently, He was able to walk on water and know what was in the hearts of people without being told (John 6:19; Matthew 9:4).

Therefore, since we have a great high priest who has gone through the heavens, Jesus the Son of God, let us hold firmly to the faith we profess. For we do not have a high priest who is unable to sympathize with our weaknesses, but we have one who has been tempted in every way, just as we are—yet was without sin. Let us then approach the throne of grace with confidence, so that we may receive mercy and find grace to help us in our time of need. (Hebrews 4:14–16)

In what ways was Jesus' experience of temptation like our own? _____

_____

_____

How did it differ? _____

_____

_____

Why should the truth of Christ's human nature be a source of encouragement to us when we experience temptation? _____

_____

_____

What should we do as a result? _____

_____

_____

Read Luke 24:36–43 and John 20:27–29, which recount two of Jesus' post-resurrection appearances. Then answer the following questions.

Jesus continues to possess a physical body in His glorified state. In what way did this provide evidence for His resurrection? _____

_____

_____

What evidence do these passages provide to indicate that Jesus continues to possess a physical body even in His resurrected and exalted state? _____

_____

_____

Why do you think Jesus showed the disciples His hands and feet? _____

_____

_____

MY RESPONSE

When Jesus appeared to the disciples after the Resurrection, He offered tangible proof of His bodily resurrection. Ignatius, an early Christian leader who served as the bishop of Antioch during the first part of the second century, noted that this proof later served as a source of courage for the disciples when they faced martyrdom for the faith. It was because of this experience, Ignatius wrote, that the disciples "despised even death" and "were proved to be above death."

1. Ignatius felt that knowing the truth about Christ's incarnation helped the early disciples face death. How might it also help us to face life? _____

_____

_____

2. What implications does the reality of Christ's physical body have for the way you treat your own body?

_____

_____

CONCLUSION

The reality of the Incarnation is one of the core truths of the Christian faith. The fact that Christ had a true human nature, including a body, is fundamental to the Bible's teaching about atonement. By taking to Himself a human nature, He has made the invisible God visible (Colossians 1:15). In Christ, "all the fullness of the Deity lives in bodily form" (Colossians 2:9). If nothing else, the reality of Christ's physical body shows us that the body does not have to be an enemy of the spiritual life. In fact, for the Christian as with Christ, spiritual life is an embodied life. Christian spirituality was meant to be expressed in the physical life of the body.

PRAYER

Read through the Gospel accounts that describe the things Christ suffered during His arrest and crucifixion, and note how many have to do with His body. Spend time thanking Christ for offering His body on your behalf and consecrate yourself to serving Him with your own body.

l e s s o n   t h r e e

THE BODY
AND THE
SOUL

KEY PASSAGE: *Do not be afraid of those who kill the body but cannot kill the soul. Rather, be afraid of the One who can destroy both soul and body in hell.*
(Matthew 10:28)

THOUGHT STARTER

When I reflect on the nature of the soul, it seems to me by far more difficult and obscure to determine its character while it is in the body, a strange domicile, than to imagine what it is when it leaves it, and has arrived in the empyreal regions, its own and proper home.
CICERO

One cannot save and then pitchfork souls into heaven. . . . Souls are more or less securely fastened to bodies . . . and as you cannot get the souls out and deal with them separately, you have to take them both together.
AMY CARMICHAEL

How does the soul differ from the body? _____

_____

_____

What does the soul have in common with the body? _____

_____

_____

Does God care less for the body than the soul? _____

_____

_____

SCRIPTURE STUDY

According to the Bible we have been created with two important dimensions to our nature: a material dimension and an immaterial dimension. The two biblical terms generally used to speak of our immaterial nature are "soul" and "spirit."

Do not be afraid of those who kill the body but cannot kill the soul. Rather, be afraid of the One who can destroy both soul and body in hell. Are not two sparrows sold for a penny? Yet not one of them will fall to the ground apart from the will of your Father. And even the very hairs of your head are all numbered. So don't be afraid; you are worth more than many sparrows. (Matthew 10:28–31)

Why should we not fear those who can kill the body? _____

_____

_____

There is a sense in which we might view the body as a container for the soul. Between these two, the soul is the more valuable part. Jesus affirmed this when He warned His disciples not to be afraid of those who can kill the body but cannot kill the soul. These words suggest that we should be more concerned about the soul than the body. Yet they do not reflect an absolute dichotomy since Jesus also links the fate of the body with that of the soul. He also affirms the Father's concern for the body. It is God's concern for me and His ultimate authority over my body that serves as the motivation for not giving in to my fear of those who can only destroy the flesh.

> *As she breathed her last [literally, "as her soul was departing"]—for she was dying—she named her son Ben-Oni. But his father named him Benjamin.* (Genesis 35:18)

> *Remember him—before the silver cord is severed, or the golden bowl is broken; before the pitcher is shattered at the spring, or the wheel broken at the well, and the dust returns to the ground it came from, and the spirit returns to God who gave it.* (Ecclesiastes 12:6–7)

> *Meanwhile, all the people were wailing and mourning for her. "Stop wailing," Jesus said. "She is not dead but asleep." They laughed at him, knowing that she was dead. But he took her by the hand and said, "My child, get up!" Her spirit returned, and at once she stood up. Then Jesus told them to give her something to eat.* (Luke 8:52–55)

> *As the body without the spirit is dead, so faith without deeds is dead.* (James 2:26)

How does the presence of the soul/spirit affect the status of the body? _____

_____

_____

What do these verses indicate is true of the soul/spirit that is not true of the body? _____

_____

_____

There is a vital connection between the material and immaterial aspects of our nature. The most obvious connection is that the soul animates the body. The fact that at death the soul or spirit returns to God while the body returns to the dust indicates that the soul can exist apart from the body. Although the body may cease to function, the soul does not. As long as the soul is present the body must be treated with the respect that is due a person. But the actions of the body also have moral and spiritual implications for the life of the soul. It is possible to use the body in a way that defiles the soul.

But I tell you that anyone who looks at a woman lustfully has already committed adultery with her in his heart. If your right eye causes you to sin, gouge it out and throw it away. It is better for you to lose one part of your body than for your whole body to be thrown into hell. And if your right hand causes you to sin, cut it off and throw it away. It is better for you to lose one part of your body than for your whole body to go into hell. (Matthew 5:28–30)

Do you think Jesus expected His disciples to disfigure themselves as a result of this command? If not, what did He want them to do? _____

_____

_____

What do these verses indicate about the spiritual implications of life in the body? _____

_____

_____

Since we have these promises, dear friends, let us purify ourselves from everything that contaminates body and spirit, perfecting holiness out of reverence for God. (2 Corinthians 7:1)

What two kinds of contamination does Paul warn us to avoid in this verse? _____

_____

_____

To what promises does this verse refer (cf. 2 Corinthians 6:16–18)? _____

_____

_____

Does Paul expect us to be "perfect"? _____

_____

_____

The perfection to which we are to aspire according to 2 Corinthians 7:1 is not sinless perfection. It is spiritual maturity reflected in growth in holiness. This maturing process begins with the recognition that God has a claim on my body. I exercise freedom in my use of my body but it does not really belong to me. The freedom I enjoy is the freedom of stewardship.

MY RESPONSE

1. What implication does the Bible's teaching about the soul/spirit have for issues like abortion and euthanasia?

_____

_____

_____

2. How should this teaching affect your view of your own body? _____

_____

_____

CONCLUSION

Ultimately it is the presence of the soul that makes me a living being and not the state of my body. Consequently, I am more than my body. This is certainly an important reminder for a culture as obsessed with body image as ours. Our sense of self-worth and the value we place on others are often directly related to physical appearance. Yet the priority of the soul and its eternal nature should force us to look beyond the state of the physical body when determining human value or defining what constitutes a "living being."

PRAYER

In Psalm 42 the Psalm writer speaks to God about the condition of his soul and the hope that he has in God. Write your own Psalm and describe the condition of your soul as you currently see it.

l e s s o n   f o u r

GOD'S PURPOSE
FOR THE
BODY

KEY PASSAGE: *Do you not know that your body is a temple of the Holy Spirit, who is in you, whom you have received from God? You are not your own; you were bought at a price. Therefore honor God with your body.* (1 Corinthians 6:19–20)

WISE WORDS

God gave me a message to deliver and a horse to ride. Alas, I killed the horse, and now I cannot deliver the message.

ROBERT MURRAY MCCHEYNE

There are two things characteristic of a temple. First, it is sacred as a dwelling-place of God, and therefore cannot be profaned with impunity. Second, the proprietorship of a temple is not in man, but in God.

CHARLES HODGE

THOUGHT STARTER

Is it possible to serve God with your mind and not your body? If not, why not? _____

_____

_____

What is God's purpose for the body? _____

_____

_____

SCRIPTURE STUDY

God has a purpose for each person's body. It is His desire that the individual use it to bring glory to Him. In Romans 6:13–14 the apostle Paul shows us what this looks like and compares our present condition with our past.

Do not offer the parts of your body to sin, as instruments of wickedness, but rather offer yourselves to God, as those who have been brought from death to life; and offer the parts of your body to him as instruments of righteousness. For sin shall not be your master, because you are not under law, but under grace. (Romans 6:13–14)

What does Paul say we should not do? _____

_____

_____

What happens when we offer the parts of our body to sin? _____

_____

_____

How should we view ourselves? _____

_____

_____

Why should this prompt us to offer the parts of our body to God as instruments of righteousness? _____

_____

_____

We can offer our bodies to sin as instruments of unrighteousness or we can present our bodies to God as instruments of righteousness. Once we are in Christ, we are no longer enslaved to sin. We can, however, continue to live in bondage to it. One of the keys to honoring God with our bodies is to see ourselves as those who are under the freedom of grace rather than the slavery of the Law.

It is God's will that you should be sanctified: that you should avoid sexual immorality; that each of you should learn to control his own body in a way that is holy and honorable, not in passionate lust like the heathen, who do not know God; and that in this matter no one should wrong his brother or take advantage of him. The Lord will punish men for all such sins, as we have already told you and warned you. For God did not call us to be impure, but to live a holy life. (1 Thessalonians 4:3–7)

How does Paul summarize what God's will is for the believer? _____

_____

_____

What practical example does he give? _____

_____

_____

What warning does he give in connection with this command? _____

_____

_____

Ultimately, God's purpose for the body is its sanctification. In particular, Paul mentions the importance of moral purity. The follower of Christ must know how to "control" the body, evaluating every action by two primary guidelines. First, is this behavior that is consistent with holiness? Secondly, is it honorable behavior? The first question looks at our behavior with God's character in view. The second question looks at it with our reputation in mind. It is not our reputation alone that is important. Since we represent Christ, our actions either honor or dishonor Him.

You, however, are controlled not by the sinful nature but by the Spirit, if the Spirit of God lives in you. And if anyone does not have the Spirit of Christ, he does not belong to Christ. But if Christ is in you, your body is dead because of sin, yet your spirit is alive because of righteousness. And if the Spirit of him who raised Jesus from the dead is living in you, he who raised Christ from the dead will also give life to your mortal bodies through his Spirit, who lives in you. Therefore, brothers, we have an obligation—but it is not to the sinful nature, to live according to it. (Romans 8:9–12)

How has sin affected the body? _____

_____

_____

What is true of us if Christ is in us? _____

_____

_____

What will this mean for our bodies in the future? _____

_____

_____

How should this affect our actions in the present? _____

_____

_____

Read 2 Corinthians 5:1–10. Then answer the following questions.

What metaphor does Paul use to refer to the physical body in these verses? _____

_____

_____

How does our "heavenly" body differ from our "earthly" body? _____

_____

_____

What guarantee has God given to assure us that we will one day be "clothed" with a new body? _____

_____

_____

As long as we are "at home in the body" we are "away from the Lord." What is true of those believers who are "away from the body"? _____

_____

_____

How should this affect our view of death? _____

_____

_____

Because the bodies we currently possess are mortal, death is inevitable. Those who know Christ as Savior do not have to dread this fate since absence from the body will mean that we are present with the Lord. The knowledge that we will appear before Christ should motivate us to use our bodies to bring glory to Him.

In 1 Corinthians 15:35–58 the apostle Paul contrasts our natural body with the body that we will have in the resurrection. Compare the two below:

	Natural Body	**Resurrection Body**
Verse 40:	_____	_____
Verse 42:	_____	_____
Verse 43:	_____	_____
Verse 44:	_____	_____
Verse 52:	_____	_____
Verse 53:	_____	_____
Verse 54:	_____	_____

According to 1 Corinthians 15:58, how should the hope of resurrection affect us in our service for Christ?

_____

_____

_____

MY RESPONSE

1. Review your actions over the past few days. Are there any for which you would find it difficult to give an account to God? _____

_____

_____

2. Which truths emphasized in today's study might have helped you to act differently? _____

_____

_____

3. What steps do you need to take in order to use the members of your body as instruments of righteousness?

_____

_____

_____

CONCLUSION

How important is the body? It is important enough to comprise the capstone of the believer's redemptive experience. The Scriptures teach that bodily resurrection is the inevitable result of being united with Christ. Consequently, our present condition is one of longing. The soul's ultimate desire is not to be a disembodied spirit, but to be "clothed" with an imperishable body. This was the purpose for which we were made. It is this hope that provides the proper theological perspective toward our earthly bodies. God's purpose for our earthly body is the same as His purpose for our "heavenly" body. Both are created for His glory. To use Paul's language, "The body is for the Lord and the Lord is for the body" (1 Corinthians 6:13).

PRAYER

Some have accused Christians of being "so heavenly minded they are no earthly good." In reality we are not heavenly minded enough. Recognizing that God has an eternal purpose for our body will motivate us to use it for His glory. Ask God to help you to be more "heavenly minded" in the way you use the members of your body for Him.

GLORIFYING
GOD WITH
YOUR BODY

KEY PASSAGE: *Therefore, I urge you, brothers, in view of God's mercy, to offer your bodies as living sacrifices, holy and pleasing to God—this is your spiritual act of worship.*
(Romans 12:1)

WISE WORDS

Take my hands and let them move
At the impulse of Thy love;
Take my feet and let them be
Swift and beautiful for Thee,
Swift and beautiful for Thee.

FRANCES RIDLEY HAVERGAL

You cannot devalue the body and value the soul—or value anything else.
WENDELL BERRY

THOUGHT STARTER

Why is the body important to the Christian life? _____

_____

_____

What would you say to someone who argued that since the body is physical and not spiritual, it does not matter how one uses it? _____

_____

_____

How important was it that Jesus had a physical body? Why? _____

_____

_____

SCRIPTURE STUDY

Paul urges believers to offer their bodies as a living sacrifice to God (Romans 12:1). This is a call to the believer to offer the whole person. Consecration to God is not a single act but a continual commitment that is expressed in very practical ways.

How are those referred to in the verses below using their eyes?

Proverbs 6:13; 16:30 _____

_____

Proverbs 6:17; 21:4 _____

_____

Proverbs 6:25 _____

_____

Proverbs 17:24 _____

_____

Proverbs 20:8 _____

_____

Matthew 5:28 _____

_____

Jesus spoke of the possibility of the eye causing one to sin (Matthew 5:29; Mark 9:47). Jesus also warned that anyone who looks at another person with lust has already committed adultery of the heart (Matthew 5:28). More often, however, the Bible warns of what the eye implies about the inner person. However, not everything the Bible says about the eyes is evil. They can be used for good as well.

Like the eye, the ear can be used for righteousness or sin. How are those referred to in the verses below using their ears?

Proverbs 2:2 _____

_____

Proverbs 21:13 _____

_____

Proverbs 23:12 _____

_____

Proverbs 28:9 _____

_____

Jeremiah 5:21 _____

_____

Matthew 11:15 _____

_____

Acts 7:51 _____

_____

A "listening ear" is one that is quick to pay attention to the lesson of a wise man's rebuke and is compared to an earring of gold (Proverbs 25:12). However, someone who turns a "deaf ear" to God's Law will find that his prayers are "detestable" (Proverbs 28:9). The prophet Jeremiah characterized the house of Jacob as a "foolish and senseless people, who have eyes but do not see, who have ears but do not hear" (Jeremiah 5:21). This was later echoed in the ministry of Christ who repeatedly urged: "He who has an ear, let him hear" (Matthew 11:15; 13:9, 43; Mark 4:9, 23; Luke 8:8; 14:35).

The tongue can be either an instrument of blessing or of cursing. How is the tongue used in the following passages?

Proverbs 10:20–21 _____

_____

Proverbs 11:12 _____

_____

Proverbs 12:18 _____

_____

Proverbs 18:21 _____

_____

Isaiah 50:4 _____

_____

James 1:26 _____

_____

When we put bits into the mouths of horses to make them obey us, we can turn the whole animal. Or take ships as an example. Although they are so large and are driven by strong winds, they are steered by a very small rudder wherever the pilot wants to go. Likewise the tongue is a small part of the body, but it makes great boasts. Consider what a great forest is set on fire by a small spark. The tongue also is a fire, a world of evil among the parts of the body. It corrupts the whole person, sets the whole course of his life on fire, and is itself set on fire by hell. (James 3:3–6)

To what three objects does James compare the tongue? _____

_____

_____

What makes the tongue so dangerous? _____

_____

_____

What do the verses listed below say about the hands and feet?

Psalm 24:4 _____

_____

Psalm 26:6 _____

_____

Proverbs 1:16 _____

_____

Proverbs 6:18 _____

_____

Romans 10:15 _____

_____

1 Thessalonians 4:11 _____

_____

Psalm 24:4 declares that only those who have "clean" hands may come into God's presence. Bloodthirsty men, however, are those "in whose hands are wicked schemes, whose right hands are full of bribes" (Psalm 26:10). Feet, like one's hands and tongue, can be used as much for evil purposes as for good. The wicked use their feet to "rush into sin" (Proverbs 1:16; 6:18). Yet they can also be used to bring the message of the gospel to others (Romans 10:15).

MY RESPONSE

1. Spend time reflecting upon your eyes, ears, mouth, hands, and feet. Choose one and think of how have you used it in the past week. _____

_____

_____

2. How did you use this member of your body to glorify God? _____

_____

_____

3. Did you use it in any way that you now regret? _____

_____

_____

CONCLUSION

The body plays an important role in the believer's spiritual life. We serve God in the body. We also serve Him with our bodies. Every member has the potential to be used to bless others and to bring glory to God. What kind of body does God prefer? It is a body that has been consecrated to His service. The primary function of the body is not to be put on display but to be offered to God as a living sacrifice. We were created to worship and serve God with our bodies. Both now and in eternity, the body is for the Lord.

PRAYER

Thank God for the potential that each member of your body has for bringing glory to God. Pray for your eyes, ears, hands, and feet and consecrate each one to God's service.

GOD'S
GYM

l e s s o n   o n e

THE GOAL OF
SPIRITUAL
TRAINING

KEY PASSAGE: *His divine power has given us everything we need for life and godliness through our knowledge of him who called us by his own glory and goodness.* (2 Peter 1:3)

WISE WORDS

Consider the necessity of holiness. It is impossible that ever you should be happy, except you are holy. No holiness here, no happiness hereafter.

THOMAS BROOKS

No voice but the voice of God can make the spiritually dead to hear, to hear so as to believe and obey.

JOHN BROWN

THOUGHT STARTER

How would you define godliness? _____

_____

_____

Why is godliness better than ungodliness? _____

_____

_____

Who is the most godly person you know? What is it that makes that person "godly"? _____

_____

_____

SCRIPTURE STUDY

The Scriptures often speak of godliness as a characteristic of the believer but do not give a detailed definition of what is meant by the term. What does a truly godly person look like? One way to answer this question is by comparing godliness to its opposite. Analyze Romans 1:18–23 to uncover some of the characteristics of godliness.

	Ungodliness is:	**Godliness is:**
Verse 18:	_____	_____
	_____	_____
Verse 19:	_____	_____
	_____	_____
Verse 20:	_____	_____
	_____	_____
Verse 21:	_____	_____
	_____	_____
Verse 22:	_____	_____
	_____	_____
Verse 23:	_____	_____
	_____	_____

Timothy, guard what has been entrusted to your care. Turn away from godless chatter and the opposing ideas of what is falsely called knowledge, which some have professed and in so doing have wandered from the faith. Grace be with you. . . . Avoid godless chatter, because those who indulge in it will become more and more ungodly. . . . Among them are Hymenaeus and Philetus, who have wandered away from the truth. They say that the resurrection has already taken place, and they destroy the faith of some. (1 Timothy 6:20–21; 2 Timothy 2:16–18)

What is Paul referring to when he speaks of "godless chatter"? _____
_____
_____

What is wrong with this kind of talk? _____
_____
_____

What does this imply about the relationship between biblical truth and godliness? _____
_____
_____

One of the primary marks of godlessness is to "suppress the truth" by unrighteous behavior. Godliness, then, must have the opposite effect. Godly behavior brings the truth to light. Godliness has its origin in God's truth. Those who occupy themselves with what Paul describes as "godless chatter" . . . "will become more and more ungodly." They will deviate from the fundamental principles of the faith. Godliness, on the other hand, is built upon the foundation of the word of truth. Knowledge of the truth leads to godliness.

Paul, a servant of God and an apostle of Jesus Christ for the faith of God's elect and the knowledge of the truth that leads to godliness—a faith and knowledge resting on the hope of eternal life, which God, who does not lie, promised before the beginning of time, and at his appointed season he brought his word to light through the preaching entrusted to me by the command of God our Savior. (Titus 1:1–3)

How does Paul describe his mission in these verses? _____

_____

_____

Upon what foundation does this knowledge rest? _____

_____

_____

What kind of impact does it have upon those who understand and accept it? _____

_____

_____

How is it learned? _____

_____

_____

When Paul describes that which has been entrusted to him as "a faith and knowledge resting on the hope of eternal life," he is not speaking of faith in the subjective sense. He is not referring to the believer's personal experience of faith but to the content of what is known and believed.

Read Genesis 25:29–34 and Hebrews 12:16–17. Then answer the following questions.

Why do you think the author of Hebrews characterizes Esau's sale of his inheritance rights as a "godless" act?

_____

_____

How did Esau react when the blessing was given to another (cf. Genesis 27:34–41)? _____

_____

_____

According to the author of Hebrews, what lesson should we learn from Esau's example? _____

_____

_____

Esau proved that he was ungodly when he sold his birthright for a single meal. He did not value God's promises. Later, when he expressed sorrow over the loss of his inheritance, it was too late. Esau was a sensualist at heart, driven by his appetite to such a degree that he was willing to sell his inheritance for a single meal. The godly person knows the value of God's promises and will not barter them for profit or pleasure, no matter how immediate either may be. In this same verse the author of Hebrews warns his readers to look carefully to make sure that no one in their midst shares Esau's godless values. This is a responsibility shared by the entire congregation. Godliness flourishes best in an environment of loving accountability.

Read Jude 4 and Titus 2:11–15. Then answer these two questions:

In what way does the godless person distort the Bible's teaching about the grace of God? _____
_____
_____

How should the experience of God's grace affect our moral lives? _____
_____
_____

MY RESPONSE

1. Do you think that others would describe you as a "godly" person? Why or why not? _____
_____
_____

2. Describe an occasion when something you learned from the Scriptures caused you to make a different moral or ethical choice than you might otherwise have made. _____
_____
_____

3. How did your experience of God's grace affect your decision? _____
_____
_____

CONCLUSION

The fact that God forgives our sin does not mean that He views sin lightly. Those who sin thinking *God will forgive me later* have distorted the biblical teaching about grace. God's grace has the opposite effect. It enables us to say no to the flesh and say yes to God. Godliness is a fruit of divine grace.

PRAYER

Think of someone you know who could be described as an "ungodly" person. Pray that they will see their need for the transforming grace of God.

OBSTACLES TO SPIRITUAL TRAINING

KEY PASSAGE: *For in my inner being I delight in God's law; but I see another law at work in the members of my body, waging war against the law of my mind and making me a prisoner of the law of sin at work within my members.*
(Romans 7:22–23)

WISE WORDS

Now as there is no disease so deadly as the plague, so there is no plague so deadly as the plague of the heart. Oh, this is a disease that none can cure but he who is the physician of souls.
THOMAS BROOKS

A slow cure, as the maxim says, is always surest. Diseases of the soul as well as those of the body come posting on horseback but leave slowly and on foot.
FRANCIS DE SALES

THOUGHT STARTER

What are some of the factors that make it difficult for some people to be disciplined in the area of physical exercise? _____

_____

_____

Why aren't good intentions enough? _____

_____

_____

Do you see a similarity in the factors that make it difficult for some Christians to be disciplined in their spiritual lives? _____

_____

_____

SCRIPTURE STUDY

Every new year many of us make the same resolution. We promise ourselves that we will eat better and get more exercise. Fitness centers report that every January they are flooded with new memberships, and their facilities are crowded with people who have decided to get in shape. After a few weeks, however, things go back to normal, and these same well-meaning promises are soon forgotten until next year when the cycle begins again. This is not unlike what happens in our spiritual lives. We resolve to be more disciplined in our spiritual lives, and we really mean it. We may even try to read the Bible or pray more. But before we know it, things are back to "normal" in our lives. We had good intentions but stumbled over unanticipated obstacles on the path to spiritual training.

Read Psalm 119:9–16. Then answer the following questions.

How did meditating on God's Word help the psalmist? _____

_____

_____

What motivated him to make the effort to "hide" God's Word in his heart, "recount" God's laws, and meditate on His precepts? _____

_____

_____

What kept him from neglecting God's Word? _____

_____

_____

One of the most common obstacles to spiritual training is simple ignorance. We do not know what we are missing. Disciplined study of God's Word had a transforming effect in the life of the psalmist, but this was not what motivated him to meditate upon it. He devoted himself to God's Word because he enjoyed it. If we think that practicing the disciplines of the spiritual life will be boring or painful, we are not going to be very eager to engage in them.

When you fast, do not look somber as the hypocrites do, for they disfigure their faces to show men they are fasting. I tell you the truth, they have received their reward in full. But when you fast, put oil on your head and wash your face, so that it will not be obvious to men that you are fasting, but only to your Father, who is unseen; and your Father, who sees what is done in secret, will reward you. (Matthew 6:16–18)

Jesus warned His disciples not to fast like the hypocrites. What was wrong with their practice of this spiritual discipline? _____

_____

_____

How does it affect our approach to spiritual training when we engage in it to be seen by others? _____

_____

_____

What counsel does Jesus offer to those who struggle with this tendency? _____

_____

_____

What causes fights and quarrels among you? Don't they come from your desires that battle within you? You want something but don't get it. You kill and covet, but you cannot have what you want. You quarrel and fight. You do not have, because you do not ask God. When you ask, you do not receive, because you ask with wrong motives, that you may spend what you get on your pleasures. (James 4:1–3)

How did false expectations affect the prayer life of those James describes in these verses? _____

_____

_____

Were they wrong to want God to answer their prayers? _____

_____

_____

What was wrong with their prayers? _____

_____

_____

James criticized His readers for praying with selfish motives. The problem was not that they wanted God to answer their prayers but that they were concerned only for their own pleasures. Their prayers were motivated by self-indulgence and jealousy, the same attitudes that had split the church in violent quarreling. James's rebuke is an important reminder that there is more to spiritual training than methodology. Motive is just as important as method.

Read the account in Mark 14:33–42 of the disciples being with Jesus in the Garden of Gethsemane. Then answer the following questions.

What did Jesus ask the disciples to do? Why? _____

_____

_____

What explanation does Jesus give for their falling asleep? _____

_____

_____

How do you think they felt after Jesus rebuked them? _____

_____

_____

Why do you think they couldn't explain their behavior to Jesus? _____

_____

_____

How might the following factors have contributed to the disciples' failure to pray at this crucial time?

Physical: _____

_____

Mental: _____

_____

Emotional: _____

_____

Spiritual: _____

_____

MY RESPONSE

1. Which of the problems facing the disciples in the Garden of Gethsemane—physical, mental, emotional, and spiritual weariness—poses the greatest obstacle to your own program of spiritual training? _____

_____

_____

2. Make a "contract" with yourself to address the problem.

The Problem: _____

_____

Steps I need to take: _____

_____

I need to do this by: _____

_____

The first thing I must do is: _____

_____

CONCLUSION

Spiritual training, like physical exercise, requires planning, effort, and discipline. Good intentions are not enough to insure that spiritual training will take place. Success requires the right information, proper motivation, and a realistic assessment of the obstacles that might hamper our progress. In fact, by analyzing our own failures, we may discover areas where changes need to be made. We may need to get more information or set more reasonable goals for ourselves. Our motives may need a major adjustment, or we may only need to take some simple practical steps (such as going to bed earlier) to remove the physical obstacles that get in the way of spiritual training.

PRAYER

Ask God to help you follow through on your plans to remove the obstacles that hinder your spiritual training. Ask Him to provide you with the right information, proper motives, and a realistic plan.

THE MEANS OF
SPIRITUAL TRAINING:
GRACE, TRUTH, AND EFFORT

KEY PASSAGE: *I pray that out of his glorious riches he may strengthen you with power through his Spirit in your inner being, so that Christ may dwell in your hearts through faith. And I pray that you, being rooted and established in love, may have power, together with all the saints, to grasp how wide and long and high and deep is the love of Christ, and to know this love that surpasses knowledge—that you may be filled to the measure of all the fullness of God.*
(Ephesians 3:16–19)

WISE WORDS

The duty is ours, but the power whereby we perform it is God's. The Spirit is the only successful combatant against the lusts that war in our members.
JOHN FLAVEL

And first of all, whatever good work you begin to do, beg of Him with most earnest prayer to perfect it.
BENEDICT OF NURSIA

THOUGHT STARTER

Why can't effort alone lead to spiritual transformation? _____

_____

_____

What is the difference between human effort and grace-empowered effort? _____

_____

_____

What role does God's truth play in spiritual transformation? _____

_____

_____

SCRIPTURE STUDY

Godliness is the goal of spiritual training, but what are the tools God uses to produce it in the believer? The primary instruments of training are three: grace, truth, and divinely empowered effort. The most important of these is the grace of God. Grace is the ground for all godliness. There is no godliness without grace.

In fact, if the foundation of God's grace is removed, the same actions that are a reflection of godliness in the believer become a form of ungodliness.

God . . . has saved us and called us to a holy life—not because of anything we have done but because of his own purpose and grace. This grace was given us in Christ Jesus before the beginning of time, but it has now been revealed through the appearing of our Savior, Christ Jesus, who has destroyed death and has brought life and immortality to light through the gospel. (2 Timothy 1:8–10).

How were we saved? _____

_____

_____

To what has God called us now that we have experienced salvation in Christ? _____

_____

_____

Teach slaves to be subject to their masters in everything, to try to please them, not to talk back to them, and not to steal from them, but to show that they can be fully trusted, so that in every way they will make the teaching about God our Savior attractive. For the grace of God that brings salvation has appeared to all men. It teaches us to say "No" to ungodliness and worldly passions, and to live self-controlled, upright and godly lives in this present age, while we wait for the blessed hope—the glorious appearing of our great God and Savior, Jesus Christ, who gave himself for us to redeem us from all wickedness and to purify for himself a people that are his very own, eager to do what is good. (Titus 2:9–14)

How did Paul expect Christian slaves to live once they had experienced the grace of God? _____

_____

_____

What would have made this command difficult to follow? _____

_____

_____

What motivation does Paul offer for obeying it? _____

_____

_____

Paul says that the grace of God "teaches" us to say no to ungodliness. What does this mean in practical terms?

_____

_____

_____

According to Paul, why did Christ give Himself for us? _____

_____

_____

Therefore, prepare your minds for action; be self-controlled; set your hope fully on the grace to be given you when Jesus Christ is revealed. As obedient children, do not conform to the evil desires you had when you lived in ignorance. But just as he who called you is holy, so be holy in all you do; for it is written: "Be holy, because I am holy." (1 Peter 1:13–16)

What kind of grace will we experience "when Jesus Christ is revealed"? _____

_____

_____

How should this expectation of future grace affect us in the present? _____

_____

_____

What does Peter say is the first step to leading a holy life? _____

_____

_____

Read James 4:4–10 and then answer the following questions.

James warns his readers those who choose to become a friend of the world become an enemy of God. What makes these two things incompatible? _____

_____

_____

How does God expect his "friends" to respond to temptation? What does He promise to do for them? _____

_____

_____

How does God want us to respond to the sin in our lives? _____

_____

_____

Holy living is an outgrowth of God's grace. The grace of God gives us the confidence to resist the flesh and the devil because it assures us that when we draw near to God in repentance, He will draw near to us. Grace is also at the root of our eagerness to see Jesus Christ return, because we expect to receive even more grace when we see Him. Grace is both a means and a motivation for living a holy life. However, as important as grace is, it does not operate alone. The handmaid of grace is truth. If there is no godliness without grace, it must also be said that there is no grace without truth. In the Christian life neither functions without the other.

The Word became flesh and made his dwelling among us. We have seen his glory, the glory of the One and Only, who came from the Father, full of grace and truth. . . . For the law was given through Moses; grace and truth came through Jesus Christ. (John 1:14, 17)

How does John summarize the ministry of Jesus in the above verses? _____

_____

_____

Read the verses below. How do they help us to understand why truth alone is not enough?

Romans 1:25 _____

_____

2 Corinthians 4:4 _____

_____

Ephesians 4:17–19 _____

_____

Colossians 2:18 _____

_____

Divinely empowered effort is the third factor that contributes to the believer's spiritual development. Human effort is as necessary to spiritual growth as grace and truth. Grace supplies the enabling power and the potential for transformation. Truth provides the direction. But what Christ has made possible must be actualized in human experience by effort.

What do the passages below say about the place of human effort in the Christian life?

1 Corinthians 15:10 _____

_____

1 Timothy 6:11–12 _____

_____

Hebrews 12:14–16 _____

_____

2 Peter 3:14 _____

_____

When is human effort incompatible with God's grace? _____

_____

_____

Effort is incompatible with grace when that effort is seen as a means of earning God's acceptance. When my efforts become the basis for my confidence with God, rather than the work of Christ, I have crossed over into the realm of legalism. In such a case, however, the problem is not with the effort itself so much as it is with the notion of earning that accompanies it. Grace and effort are compatible when grace is itself the basis for effort.

MY RESPONSE

1. In the box below, describe how grace, truth, and effort have each contributed to your spiritual growth.

Grace	Truth	Effort

2. Which of the above three areas needs more attention, if you are to continue growing spiritually? _____

_____

_____

3. How can you rely upon God's grace to a greater degree? _____

_____

_____

4. What kind of knowledge will help you to grow spiritually? _____

_____

_____

5. Where do you need to exercise the most effort in your walk with God? _____

_____

_____

CONCLUSION

Fundamentally, only the transforming power of the grace of God in Christ can explain the difference between the Christian and the unbeliever. But God's grace does not circumvent the learning process. Before we can act upon God's gracious promises we must first hear the truth about our position in Christ and our new nature. We must be taught to "put off the old self" and "put on the new" (Ephesians 4:21–24). This means that the spiritual life must of necessity also be a life of the mind.

PRAYER

Rewrite Ephesians 3:16–21 in your own words. Then speak it as a prayer. _____

_____

_____

THE METHOD OF SPIRITUAL TRAINING

KEY PASSAGE: *Have nothing to do with godless myths and old wives' tales; rather, train yourself to be godly. For physical training is of some value, but godliness has value for all things, holding promise for both the present life and the life to come.*
(1 Timothy 4:7–8)

WISE WORDS

In our era, the road to holiness necessarily passes through the world of action.
                                        DAG HAMMARSKJOLD

A baseball player who expects to excel in the game without adequate exercise of his body is no more ridiculous than the Christian who hopes to be able to act in the manner of Christ when put to the test without the appropriate exercise in godly living.
                                        DALLAS WILLARD

THOUGHT STARTER

Which spiritual disciplines have been most helpful to you? _____

_____

_____

Why have these particular disciplines been the most beneficial? _____

_____

_____

What are some of the challenges you face in the area of spiritual training? _____

_____

_____

SCRIPTURE STUDY

The secret to spiritual growth is not mere effort but effort empowered by the Holy Spirit. Living like Christ does not come automatically once we have placed our faith in the Savior. Success in the spiritual life requires prepared and sustained effort. Spiritual maturity demands training and practice. One of the ways we prepare to live the Christian life is by practicing the spiritual disciplines.

According to the following verses, what kind of practices were important to the spiritual life of Jesus?

Luke 4:16: _____

_____

Matthew 14:23: _____

_____

Luke 6:12: _____

_____

The Bible gives us only brief snapshots of the spiritual life of Jesus. Although we do not see much, what we do see reflects habits of practicing spiritual disciplines like solitude and prayer. It was His custom to participate in worship at the synagogue. These practices were an important source of spiritual strength for the Savior and provide a model for us to follow.

Have nothing to do with godless myths and old wives' tales; rather, train yourself to be godly. For physical training is of some value, but godliness has value for all things, holding promise for both the present life and the life to come. (1 Timothy 4:7–8)

What analogy does Paul use to speak of spiritual development in these verses? _____

_____

_____

What does spiritual training have in common with physical training? _____

_____

_____

How do they differ? _____

_____

_____

Do you not know that in a race all the runners run, but only one gets the prize? Run in such a way as to get the prize. Everyone who competes in the games goes into strict training. They do it to get a crown that will not last; but we do it to get a crown that will last forever. Therefore I do not run like a man running aimlessly; I do not fight like a man beating the air. No, I beat my body and make it my slave so that after I have preached to others, I myself will not be disqualified for the prize. (1 Corinthians 9:24–27)

In the passage above Paul compares his approach to his spiritual life and ministry like that of an Olympic athlete. What do the two have in common? How do they differ? Use the chart on the next page to note similarities and differences in the areas of motivation, attitude, training, and measuring success and failure.

	Athletic Training	**Christian Life**
Motivation:		
Attitude:		
Nature of Training:		
Grounds for Success or Failure:		

Therefore, since we are surrounded by such a great cloud of witnesses, let us throw off everything that hinders and the sin that so easily entangles, and let us run with perseverance the race marked out for us. Let us fix our eyes on Jesus, the author and perfecter of our faith, who for the joy set before him endured the cross, scorning its shame, and sat down at the right hand of the throne of God. Consider him who endured such opposition from sinful men, so that you will not grow weary and lose heart. In your struggle against sin, you have not yet resisted to the point of shedding your blood. (Hebrews 12:1–4)

According to the writer of Hebrews, what does the runner do to prepare for the race? _____
_____
_____

He urges his readers to rid themselves of "everything that hinders" and "the sin that so easily entangles." What is the difference between these? _____
_____
_____

What should our attitude be as we run the race of the Christian life? _____
_____
_____

What should be our focus? _____
_____
_____

Why is it important to remember that Jesus is "the author and perfecter of our faith"? _____
_____
_____

In these verses, the author of Hebrews alludes to the custom of Greek athletes who stripped down before running a race. He does this to emphasize the importance of removing any obstacles that might hinder us in living the Christian life. He also urges his readers to rid themselves of any sin that entangles them. The distinction between these two is intentional. Sin, by its nature, is a hindrance to the race. However, not everything that is a hindrance to the spiritual life is itself a sin.

MY RESPONSE

If you were to run a race with the same amount of training and effort that you devote to your spiritual life, how likely would you be to win? (Circle one.)

Highly Likely   **Somewhat Likely**   **Not Very Likely**

List some of the things that threaten to distract you from living for Christ. _____
_____
_____

How would it help you to "fix your eyes on Jesus"? _____
_____
_____

Can you think of some concrete steps that you can take to "throw off" the things that hinder you and to "run with perseverance"? _____
_____
_____

CONCLUSION

For those who struggle maintaining a regular regimen of exercise, the thought that spiritual growth demands discipline can be discouraging. The good news is that my success in practicing the spiritual disciplines is not linked to my success in being regular in physical exercise. Nor does it demand that we have a certain personality type. The secret to successful spiritual discipline is largely a matter of having the right motives and employing the right means.

PRAYER

Ask God to reveal to you the things that are hindering you in your spiritual life. Ask Him for insight to know which spiritual disciplines will help you to throw off these hindrances and focus on Jesus Christ.

l e s s o n   f i v e

FOUNDATIONAL DISCIPLINES

KEY PASSAGE: *Those who accepted his message were baptized, and about three thousand were added to their number that day. They devoted themselves to the apostles' teaching and to the fellowship, to the breaking of bread and to prayer.*
(Acts 2:41–42)

WISE WORDS

Spiritual discipline: Any activity that can help me gain power to live life as Jesus taught and modeled it.
JOHN ORTBERG

In its very nature, prayer is a confession of weakness, a confession of need, of dependence, a cry for help, a reaching out for something stronger, better, more stable and trustworthy than ourselves, on which to rest and depend and draw. No one can take this attitude once without an effect on his character; no one can take it in a crisis of his life without his whole subsequent life feeling the influence in its sweeter, humbler, more devout and restful course; no one can take it habitually without being made, merely by its natural, reflex influence, a different man, in a very profound sense, from what otherwise would have been.
B. B. WARFIELD

THOUGHT STARTER

While there are several spiritual disciplines that a believer might practice, are there any that every believer must practice? _____

_____

_____

What makes these disciplines so important to the Christian life? _____

_____

_____

How would you rank these foundational disciplines in order of their importance? Why would you place them in this order? _____

_____

_____

SCRIPTURE STUDY

Once we know that our motives are right, we must decide which disciplines will be most beneficial to our spiritual lives. There are many from which to choose. If we accept John Ortberg's definition, that a spiritual discipline is "any activity that can help me gain power to live life as Jesus taught and modeled it," then almost any action can serve as a spiritual discipline under the right circumstances. In the practice of the New Testament church, however, a few disciplines surface as being foundational to spiritual growth.

They devoted themselves to the apostles' teaching and to the fellowship, to the breaking of bread and to prayer. (Acts 2:42)

To what four practices did the New Testament believers devote themselves? _____

_____

_____

Do you think that it is significant that "the apostles' teaching" is mentioned first? _____

_____

_____

Remember how the LORD your God led you all the way in the desert these forty years, to humble you and to test you in order to know what was in your heart, whether or not you would keep his commands. He humbled you, causing you to hunger and then feeding you with manna, which neither you nor your fathers had known, to teach you that man does not live on bread alone but on every word that comes from the mouth of the LORD. (Deuteronomy 8:2–3)

Then Jesus was led by the Spirit into the desert to be tempted by the devil. After fasting forty days and forty nights, he was hungry. The tempter came to him and said, "If you are the Son of God, tell these stones to become bread." Jesus answered, "It is written: 'Man does not live on bread alone, but on every word that comes from the mouth of God.'" (Matthew 4:1–4)

Why do you think Jesus quoted Deuteronomy 8:3 when Satan challenged Him to prove His divinity by turning stones into bread? _____

_____

_____

Was Jesus minimizing the importance of food? _____

_____

_____

What do these verses imply about the importance of God's Word to our spiritual health? _____

_____

_____

All Scripture is God-breathed and is useful for teaching, rebuking, correcting and training in righteousness, so that the man of God may be thoroughly equipped for every good work. (2 Timothy 3:16–17)

Where did the Scriptures originate? _____

_____

_____

What does the phrase "God breathed" imply about the Scriptures? _____

_____

_____

Paul mentions four primary functions of God's Word. What are they? _____

_____

_____

What benefit do we gain from our study of God's Word? _____

_____

_____

The second practice of the early church mentioned in Acts 2:42 is "fellowship." In today's context this term is often used in a way that is synonymous with socializing. For example, when we have donuts and coffee after the morning service we say that we are "having fellowship." The biblical concept of fellowship is broader than this. The Greek term literally means "sharing."

What is shared in each of the verses below?

Acts 2:44–45 _____

_____

1 Corinthians 14:26 _____

_____

Galatians 2:9 _____

_____

1 John 1:3–7 _____

_____

The fellowship that believers have with Christ and with one another is symbolized in the observance of the Lord's Supper. This is probably what is signified by the phrase "breaking of bread" in Acts 2:42. The early church sometimes observed the Lord's Supper in connection with a communal meal (1 Corinthians 11:20–21; cf. Luke 24:35). According to the verses listed below, what does this observance signify?

Luke 22:19–20 _____

_____

1 Corinthians 11:24–25 _____

_____

1 Corinthians 5:7 _____

_____

How should we prepare to observe the Lord's Supper, according to 1 Corinthians 11:28? _____

_____

_____

The fourth foundational discipline mentioned in Acts 2:42 is "prayer." Saying that prayer is one of the means that God uses to promote spiritual growth in the believer is a little like saying that breathing is one of the means used to keep us alive. It is so obvious one might think that it hardly needs to be mentioned. Yet few believers are really satisfied with their prayer life. Perhaps this is because we feel that something so necessary must be easy. Prayer, however, does not always come automatically or easily, even to those who know its importance.

> *And pray in the Spirit on all occasions with all kinds of prayers and requests. With this in mind, be alert and always keep on praying for all the saints. Pray also for me, that whenever I open my mouth, words may be given me so that I will fearlessly make known the mystery of the gospel.* (Ephesians 6:18–19)

How are we to pray? _____

_____

_____

For whom should we pray? _____

_____

_____

> *Be joyful always; pray continually; give thanks in all circumstances, for this is God's will for you in Christ Jesus.* (1 Thessalonians 5:16–18)

How would the habit of continual prayer differ from prayer practiced as a discipline? _____

_____

_____

Why do you think Paul draws a connection between joy, thanksgiving, and prayer? _____

_____

_____

Read James 5:13–18; then answer the following questions.

What kinds of prayers does James describe in these verses? _____

_____

_____

Why should we be encouraged by Elijah's prayer life? _____

_____

_____

What do we have in common with Elijah? _____

_____

_____

This is the confidence we have in approaching God: that if we ask anything according to his will, he hears us. And if we know that he hears us—whatever we ask—we know that we have what we asked of him. (1 John 5:14–15)

What promise does John make about prayer in these verses? _____

_____

Why is the qualifying phrase "according to his will" important? _____

_____

Should this make us reluctant to pray? Why not? _____

_____

MY RESPONSE

1. How are you currently practicing the four foundational disciplines mentioned in Acts 2:42?

The Apostles' Teaching: _____

_____

Fellowship: _____

_____

The Breaking of Bread: _____

_____

Prayer: _____

_____

2. If any of these are missing in your life at this time, what do you need to do to begin practicing them on a regular basis? _____

_____

3. Can you think of some other practices that would help you in your Christian life? _____

_____

CONCLUSION

The history of the church demonstrates that the use of "spiritual exercises" often degenerates into a works-based approach to the Christian life. When the disciplines are removed from the context of grace and divine empowerment, they become spiritually toxic. Practicing the disciplines helps to prepare for the challenges of discipleship. They are not themselves essence of discipleship. Being a disciple is first and foremost a matter of having a relationship with Jesus Christ.

PRAYER:

Make one of the four foundational practices mentioned in Acts 2:42 the focus of your prayer. Thank God for it and ask Him to give you insight into ways that you can engage in it more effectively.

u n i t   e i g h t

CHRISTIAN
VIRTUES

PREREQUISITES
TO SPIRITUAL
MATURITY

KEY PASSAGE: *Not that I have already obtained all this, or have already been made perfect, but I press on to take hold of that for which Christ Jesus took hold of me.*
(Philippians 3:12)

WISE WORDS

Virtue is a kind of health, beauty and habit of the soul.
PLATO

No, there is no escape. There is no heaven with a little of hell in it—no plan to retain this or that of the devil in our hearts or our pockets. Out Satan must go, every hair and feather.
GEORGE MacDONALD

THOUGHT STARTER

What are the prerequisites to attaining spiritual maturity? _____

_____

_____

What must God do for us if this is to be achieved? _____

_____

_____

What must we do? _____

_____

_____

SCRIPTURE STUDY

It was he who gave some to be apostles, some to be prophets, and some to be evangelists, and some to be pastors and teachers, to prepare God's people for works of service, so that the body of Christ may be built up until we all reach unity in the faith and in the knowledge of the Son of God and become mature, attaining to the whole measure of the fullness of Christ. Then we will no longer be infants, tossed back and forth by the waves, and blown here and there by every wind of teaching and by the cunning and craftiness of men in their deceitful scheming. Instead, speaking the truth in love, we will in all things grow up into him who is the Head, that is, Christ. (Ephesians 4:11–15)

What is God's ultimate goal for the church? _____

_____

_____

What provisions has He made for this? _____

_____

_____

Paul lists several characteristics of spiritual maturity in these verses. What are they? _____

_____

_____

Now we are children of God, and what we will be has not yet been made known. But we know that when he appears, we shall be like him, for we shall see him as he is. Everyone who has this hope in him purifies himself, just as he is pure. (1 John 3:2–3)

What, according to John, is the believer's ultimate destiny? _____

_____

_____

How does this affect our present behavior? _____

_____

_____

How does this help us to answer the question: "What does spiritual maturity look like?" _____

_____

_____

According to Ephesians 4:13, God's ultimate goal for the Christian is to "become mature" which is further defined as having "the whole measure of the fullness of Christ." This is what we will look like at the end of our redemptive experience. When we ask ourselves what spiritual maturity looks like, the answer is that Christ Himself is the standard. The maturing process, then, is the experience of transformation during which, through Christ's power, we develop the character traits of Christ. Because the ultimate goal is for our lives to reflect more of Christ than of ourselves, the first prerequisite to spiritual maturity is humility.

Then Jesus said to his disciples, "If anyone would come after me, he must deny himself and take up his cross and follow me. For whoever wants to save his life will lose it, but whoever loses his life for me will find it. What good will it be for a man if he gains the whole world, yet forfeits his soul? Or what can a man give in exchange for his soul? (Matthew 16:24–26)

What did Jesus mean when He said that the one who would follow Him must "deny himself"? _____

_____

_____

What incentive did Jesus offer in these verses? _____

_____

_____

Blessed are the poor in spirit, for theirs is the kingdom of heaven. Blessed are those who mourn, for they will be comforted. Blessed are the meek, for they will inherit the earth. (Matthew 5:3–5)

What blessings does Jesus promise to the poor in spirit, those who mourn, and the meek? _____

_____

_____

How does each of these blessings resolve the spiritual condition of those who receive them? _____

_____

_____

Those who recognize their poverty of spirit know that the only way to obtain the kingdom of heaven is to receive it as a gift. Being poor in spirit begins when we declare spiritual bankruptcy and turn to Christ. But it also demands that we turn the management of our lives over to Christ. This recognition of my spiritual poverty leads to spiritual mourning. It causes me to grieve over my sinfulness and in turn produces within me the kind of humility that is reflected in meekness.

Read Philippians 3:3–9. Then answer the following questions.

When the apostle Paul described his background, he said that if anyone had reason to put confidence in the flesh, he did. What did he mean by this? _____

_____

_____

Although we may not have the same religious background as Paul, there are many things that people rely upon instead of Jesus Christ. What are some of the most common? _____

_____

_____

What did Paul eventually realize about those things he had been relying on to make him righteous before God? _____

_____

_____

How is Paul a good example of the kind of poverty of spirit, spiritual mourning, and meekness that Jesus describes in the Sermon on the Mount? _____

_____

_____

MY RESPONSE

1. When did you first recognize your own spiritual poverty and need for the righteousness of Christ? _____

_____

_____

2. What kinds of things did you come to consider "loss" for the sake of Christ? _____

_____

_____

3. Can you think of some concrete ways you can express to God your sorrow over sin? _____

_____

_____

CONCLUSION

When John the Baptist was told that Jesus' popularity had begun to outstrip his own, he rejoiced at the news. He told his followers, "He must become greater; I must become less" (John 3:30). The apostle Paul expressed a similar view when he said that he was willing to consider all of his previous achievements a loss for the sake of knowing Christ (Philippians 3:8). The most basic prerequisite to spiritual maturity is an attitude of being willing to allow Christ to transform us. There is a loss involved in this, but it is a good one. Those who submit to the transforming grace of Christ will lose all that is not a reflection of Christ. In the end, however, they will gain far more as they are changed into His image.

PRAYER

Choose one area in your life where you need to experience the "loss" and corresponding "gain" of being made more like Christ. Ask God to work in that area this week.

l e s s o n   t w o

MERCY
AND PURITY

KEY PASSAGE: *As obedient children, do not conform to the evil desires you had when you lived in ignorance. But just as he who called you is holy, so be holy in all you do; for it is written: "Be holy, because I am holy."*

(1 Peter

1:14–16)

WISE WORDS

Who knows what sort of life would result if we had attained to purity? If I knew so wise a man as could teach me purity I would seek him forthwith.

HENRY DAVID THOREAU

Nothing could more surely convince me of God's unending mercy than the continued existence on earth of the church.

ANNIE DILLARD

THOUGHT STARTER

The life of Christ is a good example of how compelling a life of purity can be. What was it about the way Jesus lived that drew so many to Him? _____

_____

_____

Can you think of other Christians to whom you have been drawn because of the purity of their lives? _____

_____

_____

Would others say this is true of you? Why or why not? _____

_____

_____

SCRIPTURE STUDY

In the Sermon on the Mount, Jesus emphasized the importance of mercy, purity of heart, and peacemaking. These traits are all reflections of God's own character. Because of this, they are not virtues we can "attain" by sheer force of will, but are graces that must be implanted within us by God Himself. They are an outgrowth of the first four beatitudes, which focus primarily on our need. Mercy, purity of heart, and peace-making are their positive counterparts because they are reflections of God's own attributes.

Which of these three attributes of mercy, purity, and peacemaking are reflected in the passages below? What do they tell you about the character of God?

Exodus 33:19 _____

_____

Psalm 119:132 _____

_____

Proverbs 28:13 _____

_____

1 John 3:1–3 _____

_____

2 Corinthians 5:18–19 _____

_____

Colossians 1:19–23 _____

_____

Read 1 Peter 2:19–25. Then answer the following questions.

How were these three characteristics of mercy, purity of heart, and peacemaking reflected in Christ's life and ministry? _____

_____

_____

What impact does this have on those who have been reconciled to God through Christ's work? _____

_____

_____

In what difficult circumstance does Peter say believers need to have a clear understanding of Christ's mercy, purity of heart, and His ministry of reconciliation? _____

_____

_____

Why would such an understanding help those who are suffering unjustly? _____

_____

_____

Make a tree good and its fruit will be good, or make a tree bad and its fruit will be bad, for a tree is recognized by its fruit. You brood of vipers, how can you who are evil say anything good? For out of the overflow of the heart the mouth speaks. The good man brings good things out of the good stored up in him, and the evil man brings evil things out of the evil stored up in him. . . . For out of the heart come evil thoughts, murder, adultery, sexual immorality, theft, false testimony, slander. (Matthew 12:33–35; 15:19)

Is Christian character merely a matter of doing the right thing? _____

_____

_____

What must be changed first before our actions can change? _____

_____

_____

How does this change take place? _____

_____

_____

The root of true holiness is ultimately a matter of the heart. When we speak, our words reflect the status of the heart. The heart is the root of all behavior, whether it is good or evil: "For out of the heart come evil thoughts, murder, adultery, sexual immorality, theft, false testimony, slander" (Matthew 15:19; cf. Luke 8:15). The starting place, then, for all those actions that are marks of spiritual maturity is a heart that has been transformed by the grace of Christ.

MY RESPONSE

1. Can you think of a time recently when you were able to show mercy to someone, or when your actions reflected purity of heart, or you were able to function as a peacemaker? List the situation(s).

_____

_____

_____

2. Think of a concrete circumstance in your life where each of these traits is currently needed, and describe in practical terms how you plan to demonstrate each.

Mercy: _____

_____

Purity of Heart: _____

_____

Peacemaking: _____

_____

CONCLUSION

God is gracious and compassionate and calls His people to exercise compassion toward others (Exodus 22:27). He is a holy God who calls His people to be holy (Leviticus 11:44–45). Yet He is also a God who shows mercy. Peacemaking, although it is an action, is also a reflection of the character of God. God is the source of peace for His people (Psalm 4:8; 29:11). Colossians 1:20 says that it was the Father's good pleasure to reconcile us through Christ "by making peace through his blood, shed on the cross."

PRAYER

Pray the following prayer, attributed to Francis of Assisi:

Lord make me an instrument of Thy peace,
Where there is hatred, let me sow love;
Where there is doubt, faith;
Where there is despair, hope;
Where there is darkness, light; and
Where there is sadness, joy.
O Divine Master, grant that I may not so much
Seek to be consoled, as to console;
To be understood as to understand;
To be loved as to love;
For it is in giving that we receive;
It is in pardoning that we are pardoned; and
It is in dying that we are born to eternal life.

LOVE,
JOY,
AND PEACE

KEY PASSAGE: *But the fruit of the Spirit is love, joy, peace. . . . Against such things there is no law.* (Galatians 5:22–23)

WISE WORDS

In order that we might receive that love whereby we should love, we were ourselves loved, while as yet we had it not.

AUGUSTINE

God cannot endure that unfestive, mirthless attitude of ours in which we eat our bread in sorrow, with pretentious, busy haste, or even with shame. Through our daily meals He is calling us to rejoice, to keep holiday in the midst of our working day.

DIETRICH BONHOEFFER

The Bible nowhere calls upon men to go out in search of peace of mind. It does call upon men to go out in search of God and the things of God.

ABBA HILLEL SILVER

THOUGHT STARTER

Paul uses the term "fruit" to describe the list of Christian virtues in Galatians 5:22–23. What does this imply about how these characteristics are produced in the life of the believer? _____

_____

_____

The first three fruits of the Spirit that Paul mentions are love, joy, and peace. Some have seen an intentional progression in this order. How are these three traits linked? _____

_____

_____

SCRIPTURE STUDY

The Beatitudes pronounce a blessing on those who exhibit foundational spiritual characteristics, but they do not say directly how those characteristics are developed. Paul's list in Galatians 5:22–23, on the other hand, roots the believer's character in the work of the Holy Spirit. Paul calls love, joy, peace, patience, kindness, goodness, faithfulness, gentleness, and self-control "the fruit of the Spirit." The fact that he refers to them as spiritual "fruit" contrasts them with the acts (literally "works") of the sinful nature described in the preceding verses (Galatians 5:19–21). This difference in language underscores a fundamental difference in their origin. The acts of the sinful nature, or our "flesh" (NASB), are self-generated. They are the natural result of the sinful nature. The characteristics that Paul describes as the fruit of the Spirit, on the other hand, have a supernatural origin. The Holy Spirit produces them.

Therefore, since we have been justified through faith, we have peace with God through our Lord Jesus Christ, through whom we have gained access by faith into this grace in which we now stand. And we rejoice in the hope of the glory of God. Not only so, but we also rejoice in our sufferings, because we know that suffering produces perseverance; perseverance, character; and character, hope. And hope does not disappoint us, because God has poured out his love into our hearts by the Holy Spirit, whom he has given us. (Romans 5:1–5)

Where does the peace spoken of in this verse originate? _____

_____

_____

What does this peace with God produce within the believer? Why? _____

_____

_____

Why shouldn't we expect the fruit of joy to disappear when our circumstances become difficult? _____

_____

_____

What is the difference between experiencing joy in the midst of trouble and enjoying trouble? _____

_____

_____

For in Christ Jesus neither circumcision nor uncircumcision has any value. The only thing that counts is faith expressing itself through love. (Galatians 5:6)

How does Paul describe the relationship between faith and love? _____

_____

_____

How should we be demonstrating our faith in Christ? _____

_____

_____

You, my brothers, were called to be free. But do not use your freedom to indulge the sinful nature; rather, serve one another in love. The entire law is summed up in a single command: "Love your neighbor as yourself." (Galatians 5:13–14)

Why might love be described as the cornerstone virtue of the Christian life? _____

_____

_____

Love is both something that we experience and something that we demonstrate. It is our experience of God's love for us that motivates us to show this same love to others. Both the subjective experience of God's love and the Christian's practice of loving others are the result of the Holy Spirit's work. The love of God is "poured out" into our hearts by the Holy Spirit" (Romans 5:5). The Holy Spirit also empowers us to show God's love to others (Colossians 1:8).

And now, brothers, we want you to know about the grace that God has given the Macedonian churches. Out of the most severe trial, their overflowing joy and their extreme poverty welled up in rich generosity. For I testify that they gave as much as they were able, and even beyond their ability. Entirely on their own, they urgently pleaded with us for the privilege of sharing in this service to the saints. . . They gave themselves first to the Lord and then to us in keeping with God's will. (2 Corinthians 8:1–5)

How did grace, joy, and obedience work together when the Macedonian churches contributed to the needs of the poor believers in Jerusalem? _____

_____

_____

Who was blessed by this act of generosity? _____

_____

_____

Read Philippians 1:21–26. Then answer the following questions.

Although Paul would have preferred to be with Christ, why was he convinced that he would remain in the body for some time yet? _____

_____

_____

How would this affect the Philippians' joy? _____

_____

_____

What is the source of joy in the verses below?

Luke 17:15 _____

_____

John 8:56 _____

_____

John 4:36 _____

_____

Acts 8:39 _____

_____

1 Thessalonians 1:6 _____

_____

1 Thessalonians 2:19–20 _____

_____

1 Thessalonians 3:9 _____

_____

James 1:2 _____

_____

1 Peter 1:8–9 _____

_____

Joy is more than a mood. Our moods are largely dependent upon external factors. While our experiences and circumstances can be an occasion for joy, they are not the ultimate source of joy. Joy is a product of the Holy Spirit. Like love, it is something that we both experience and express. We express God-given joy through worship.

Peace I leave with you; my peace I give you. I do not give to you as the world gives. Do not let your hearts be troubled and do not be afraid. . . . I have told you these things, so that in me you may have peace. In this world you will have trouble. But take heart! I have overcome the world. (John 14:27; 16:33)

What does Jesus say is different about the peace He gives to His disciples? _____

_____

_____

As a prisoner for the Lord, then, I urge you to live a life worthy of the calling you have received. Be completely humble and gentle; be patient, bearing with one another in love. Make every effort to keep the unity of the Spirit through the bond of peace. (Ephesians 4:1–3)

How does the peace Paul speaks of in this verse differ from the peace Jesus promised to His disciples? _____

_____

_____

What is required in order to preserve the unity of the Spirit in the corporate life of the church? _____

_____

_____

The spiritual fruit of peace, like joy, does not depend upon one's circumstances. Jesus promised to give His disciples a peace that differed from the world's peace. Because the peace of Christ is rooted in Christ's victory over the world, it is a peace that the world cannot shatter. It has two dimensions: peace with God and the peace of God. The latter grows out of the former. We experience true inner peace because we know that we are at peace with God. It is also the basis for effort at maintaining peace with one another in the body of Christ. We strive to preserve the "unity of the church in the bond of peace" because the peace we enjoy through Christ has joined us together in one body.

MY RESPONSE

1. In what ways has the experience of God's love, joy, and peace made a difference in your life? _____

_____

_____

2. Why would the experience of joy help you to resist temptation? _____

_____

_____

3. How can you cultivate joy in your life? What specific steps do you need to take in order to begin doing this?

_____

_____

_____

4. In what circumstance do you most need to experience the peace of God right now? _____

_____

_____

CONCLUSION

The fact that these first three fruits of the Spirit are focused on God is a needed reminder that virtue in the Christian life is a matter of being before it is a matter of doing. The moral quality of our lives is a direct result of our experience of God's love and grace. It is because we know and have experienced the love of God that we have a sense of joy that cannot be diminished by our circumstances. That love is communicated to us in our innermost being by the Holy Spirit, who gives us peace and helps us to live in peace with one another.

PRAYER

Read Romans 15:13, Ephesians 3:16–21, and 1 Thessalonians 5:23 and use them as the basis for prayer. Ask God to allow you to experience more of His love, joy, and peace.

PATIENCE,
KINDNESS,
AND GOODNESS

KEY PASSAGE: *But the fruit of the Spirit is . . . patience, kindness, goodness.*
(Galatians 5:22)

WISE WORDS

All men commend patience, although few be willing to practice it.
THOMAS 'A KEMPIS

More people have been brought into the church by the kindness of real Christian love than by all the theological arguments in the world, and more people have been driven from the church by the hardness and ugliness of so-called Christianity than by all the doubts in the world.
WILLIAM BARCLAY

As a rule, prayer is answered and funds come in, but if we are kept waiting, the spiritual blessing that is the outcome is far more precious than exemption from the trial.
J. HUDSON TAYLOR

THOUGHT STARTER

What do patience, kindness, and goodness have in common? _____

_____

_____

Is it possible to have one without the others? _____

_____

_____

Think of someone who exhibits these traits. How does that person show them? _____

_____

_____

SCRIPTURE STUDY

The second triad of virtues mentioned in Galatians 5:22–23 is made up of characteristics that have an outward focus. They are patience, kindness, and goodness. All three are reflected in our treatment of others and are characteristics of God Himself. We exercise patience and demonstrate kindness and goodness because we have experienced these things through Christ.

Then the LORD came down in the cloud and stood there with him and proclaimed his name, the LORD. And he passed in front of Moses, proclaiming, "The LORD, the LORD, the compassionate and gracious God, slow to anger, abounding in love and faithfulness, maintaining love to thousands, and forgiving wickedness, rebellion and sin. Yet he does not leave the guilty unpunished; he punishes the children and their children for the sin of the fathers to the third and fourth generation." (Exodus 34:5–7)

How is God's patience a product of His kindness and goodness? _____

_____

_____

Does the fact that God is patient mean that He ignores sin? _____

_____

_____

The Lord is not slow in keeping his promise, as some understand slowness. He is patient with you, not wanting anyone to perish, but everyone to come to repentance. (2 Peter 3:9)

Even though I was once a blasphemer and a persecutor and a violent man, I was shown mercy because I acted in ignorance and unbelief. The grace of our Lord was poured out on me abundantly, along with the faith and love that are in Christ Jesus. Here is a trustworthy saying that deserves full acceptance: Christ Jesus came into the world to save sinners—of whom I am the worst. But for that very reason I was shown mercy so that in me, the worst of sinners, Christ Jesus might display his unlimited patience as an example for those who would believe on him and receive eternal life. (1 Timothy 1:13–16)

Why, according to Peter, does God exercise patience? _____

_____

_____

How was the apostle Paul a prime example of this? _____

_____

_____

In what ways has your own experience reflected this? _____

_____

_____

As a prisoner for the Lord, then, I urge you to live a life worthy of the calling you have received. Be completely humble and gentle; be patient, bearing with one another in love. Make every effort to keep the unity of the Spirit through the bond of peace. (Ephesians 4:1–3)

Why is patience needed to maintain the unity in the church? _____

_____

_____

In what kind of situations do you think patience is most needed? _____

_____

_____

Since the church is made up of those who are in a variety of stages in their spiritual growth, there will be plenty of opportunities for aggravation, hurt, and mutual disappointment between believers. There is a sense in which we have been called to "put up with one another" in the body of Christ. This is to be done in an attitude of love rather than in a condescending manner. However, since we are self-centered by nature, it must also be done in the power of the Holy Spirit.

And God raised us up with Christ and seated us with him in the heavenly realms in Christ Jesus, in order that in the coming ages he might show the incomparable riches of his grace, expressed in his kindness to us in Christ Jesus. (Ephesians 2:6–7)

At one time we too were foolish, disobedient, deceived and enslaved by all kinds of passions and pleasures. We lived in malice and envy, being hated and hating one another. But when the kindness and love of God our Savior appeared, he saved us, not because of righteous things we had done, but because of his mercy. He saved us through the washing of rebirth and renewal by the Holy Spirit, whom he poured out on us generously through Jesus Christ our Savior. (Titus 3:3–6)

What did God do to demonstrate His kindness toward us? _____

_____

_____

Why was this the ultimate expression of kindness? _____

_____

_____

How did it make kindness possible for us? _____

_____

_____

What is the difference between patience and kindness? How are they similar? _____

_____

_____

Patience is essentially a passive quality. It refrains from taking action. Kindness is its active counterpart. Kindness is demonstrated to others. God's kindness is not limited to believers only—He shows kindness even to those who do not appreciate it and to those who do not deserve it. His ultimate act of kindness was in showing grace to us through His son, Jesus Christ. Those who have experienced God's kindness have an obligation to show kindness to others.

As Jesus started on his way, a man ran up to him and fell on his knees before him. "Good teacher," he asked, "what must I do to inherit eternal life?" "Why do you call me good?" Jesus answered. "No one is good—except God alone. (Mark 10:17–18)

If no one is good except God alone, how is it possible for us to exhibit the fruit of goodness? _____

_____

_____

What did the man described in these verses need to recognize about Jesus? _____

_____

_____

What did he need to recognize about himself (cf. Mark 10:19–27)? _____

_____

_____

You were once darkness, but now you are light in the Lord. Live as children of light (for the fruit of the light consists in all goodness, righteousness and truth) and find out what pleases the Lord. (Ephesians 5:8–10)

In Ephesians 5:9 the apostle Paul characterizes goodness as a "fruit of the light." Why do you think he describes it this way? _____

_____

_____

With what other attributes is goodness linked in this passage? _____

_____

_____

How does this help you to understand the nature of biblical goodness? _____

_____

_____

Our people must learn to devote themselves to doing what is good, in order that they may provide for daily necessities and not live unproductive lives. (Titus 3:14)

In this verse Paul says that those who devote themselves to doing what is good should do so in order to provide for "daily necessities." What does this tell you about the ordinary context of "doing good" in the Christian life?

_____

_____

Where will we have an opportunity to "do good" most often? _____

_____

_____

Goodness is what kindness looks like in action. It involves more than simply being good; it is reflected in the believer's life by doing good to others. The spiritual fruit of goodness is demonstrated in a generous spirit. We can show generosity in the way we handle our finances, but it is not limited to this realm. Those who possess the fruit of goodness show a sympathetic interest in others and are as concerned about the well-being and advancement of others as they are about their own. It is the same attitude described in Philippians 2:3–4: "Do nothing out of selfish ambition or vain conceit, but in humility consider others better than yourselves. Each of you should look not only to your own interests, but also to the interests of others."

MY RESPONSE

1. Next to each fruit of the Spirit listed below write the name of someone to whom you can show that characteristic and describe how it can be done.

	Who Can I Show It to?	**How Can I Show It?**
Patience		
Kindness		
Goodness		

CONCLUSION

Patience, kindness, and goodness are more than moral virtues. They are a reflection of God's own attributes and actions. When we exercise these virtues, we are not merely trying to be good. We are trying to be like God. That is why we are dependent upon the power of God's Spirit to produce these qualities in us. When we are patient, kind, and good, it is because God is showing His patience, kindness, and goodness through us. Through the Spirit we become channels of God's love.

PRAYER

Choose one of the people you noted above to whom you want to model God's patience, kindness, or goodness. Ask God to give you an opportunity to do so, and pray for your own response when it comes.

SPIRIT-CONTROLLED SELF-MASTERY

KEY PASSAGE: *But the fruit of the Spirit is . . . faithfulness, gentleness and self-control.*
(Galatians 5:22–23)

WISE WORDS

We are not masters of our own feeling, but we are by God's grace masters of our consent.
FRANCOIS FENELON

We live under the illusion that if we can acquire complete control, we can understand God, or we can write the great American novel. But the only way we can brush against the hem of the Lord, or hope to be part of the creative process, is to have the courage, the faith, to abandon control. For the opposite of sin is faith, and never virtue, and we live in a world which believes that self-control can make us virtuous. But that's not how it works.

MADELEINE L'ENGLE

THOUGHT STARTER

Why do you think Madeleine L'Engle says that faith rather than virtue is the opposite of sin? _____

_____

_____

Given the reality of our sinful nature, is self-control a realistic goal for the Christian? _____

_____

_____

SCRIPTURE STUDY

The third triad of spiritual virtues in Galatians 5:22–23 lists characteristics that show evidence of Spirit-controlled self-mastery. The first of these, translated "faithfulness," is actually the word "faith" in the Greek text. The context, however, suggests that in this case Paul is not thinking of faith in God but of reliable or dependable character on the part of the believer. This is the characteristic of Spirit-enabled consistency. Like the other characteristics in this list, faithfulness is an attribute of God.

Know therefore that the LORD your God is God; he is the faithful God, keeping his covenant of love to a thousand generations of those who love him and keep his commands. But those who hate him he will repay to their face by destruction; he will not be slow to repay to their face those who hate him. Therefore, take care to follow the commands, decrees and laws I give you today. . . . He is the Rock, his works are perfect, and all his ways are just. A faithful God who does no wrong, upright and just is he. (Deuteronomy 7:9–11; 32:4)

How does God show that He is faithful? _____

_____

_____

How does He expect His people to reflect His own faithful character? _____

_____

_____

For the word of the Lord is right and true; he is faithful in all he does. (Psalm 33:4)

By what standard did the psalmist measure God's actions in order to conclude that He is faithful in all He does? _____

_____

_____

May God himself, the God of peace, sanctify you through and through. May your whole spirit, soul and body be kept blameless at the coming of our Lord Jesus Christ. The one who calls you is faithful and he will do it. (1 Thessalonians 5:23–24)

Here is a trustworthy saying: If we died with him, we will also live with him; if we endure, we will also reign with him. If we disown him, he will also disown us; if we are faithless, he will remain faithful, for he cannot disown himself. (2 Timothy 2:11–13)

Why should God's faithfulness be the basis for the believer's assurance of salvation? _____

_____

_____

Is God's faithfulness to His promises contingent upon our performance? _____

_____

_____

Read the verses below and note what kind of faithfulness God expects from those who know Christ as Savior.

Matthew 5:37: _____

_____

Romans 15:7: _____

_____

Ephesians 4:3: _____

_____

When faithfulness is shown to others, it takes the form of loyalty. Loyalty prompts us to deal truthfully with others, but gentleness is also needed in order to be considerate in the way that I speak the truth. It is no surprise, then, that in his list of the fruit of the Spirit in Galatians 5:22–23 Paul associates faithfulness with gentleness.

> *Brothers, if someone is caught in a sin, you who are spiritual should restore him gently. But watch yourself, or you also may be tempted. Carry each other's burdens, and in this way you will fulfill the law of Christ.* (Galatians 6:1–2)

Why is gentleness needed when restoring someone who has been caught in a sin? _____

_____

_____

How will thinking of ourselves help us to be gentle when dealing with such a person? _____

_____

_____

Gentleness does not come to us automatically. We must choose the path of gentleness when dealing with others. It is especially important when dealing with others who are caught in sin. Dealing gently with those who have fallen and are repentant is really just a matter of treating others the way we ourselves would want to be treated.

Read Romans 6:16–18. Then answer the following questions.

How do these verses say that we should view ourselves? _____

_____

_____

Why would such a perspective help us to exercise self-control? _____

_____

_____

> *Those who belong to Christ Jesus have crucified the sinful nature with its passions and desires. Since we live by the Spirit, let us keep in step with the Spirit.* (Galatians 5:24–25)

What must those who want to live by the Spirit recognize about their sinful nature? _____

_____

_____

How will this recognition help them to "keep in step" with the Spirit? _____

_____

_____

MY RESPONSE

1. Describe a situation in your life where the fruit of faithfulness is needed. _____

_____

_____

2. Describe a situation in your life where the fruit of gentleness is needed. _____

_____

_____

3. Describe a situation in your life where the fruit of self-control is needed. _____

_____

_____

4. Rate yourself in showing these three virtues from 1–5, with 1 being weakest and 5 being the strongest.

Faithfulness

   1   2   3   4   5

Gentleness

   1   2   3   4   5

Self-control

   1   2   3   4   5

CONCLUSION

The alternative to a life governed by Spirit-controlled self-mastery is bondage (Romans 6:16; 2 Peter 2:19). The fruit of self-control is much more than the decision to "just say no." It is a moment-by-moment application of the Cross to our affections, thoughts, and actions. Every time we exercise self-control we declare with our lives the gospel truth that through Christ our sinful nature has been crucified along with its passions and desires. We say no to the flesh and yes to God. Ultimately, this is what it means to walk in the Spirit.

PRAYER

Choose one of the areas you rated above and plan the next step that needs to be taken in order to improve in this area. Pray for the enabling power of the Holy Spirit to help you to follow through on your plans.

THE
SPIRITUAL
JOURNEY

CALLED
TO FOLLOW
CHRIST

KEY PASSAGE: *"Come, follow me," Jesus said, "and I will make you fishers of men."*
(Mark 1:17)

WISE WORDS

Yes, Christ takes complete fools, both uneducated and ignorant of doctrine as subjects for his fine training, for renewal by the grace of his Spirit, that they may excel all the wise men of the world. This is how he wished to put down the pride of the flesh, of course, and to make in the person of these men an outstanding example of spiritual grace, that we might learn to seek the light of faith from heaven, knowing that we cannot acquire it by our own industry.

JOHN CALVIN

When the Spirit, revealing the will of God for the world, creates in the heart a great pain and a great discontent, do not check it.

G. CAMPBELL MORGAN

THOUGHT STARTER

Which do you enjoy most when you take a trip, the journey or reaching the destination? Why? _____

_____

_____

Is there anything that makes you anxious prior to setting out? _____

_____

_____

In what ways is the Christian life like a journey? _____

_____

_____

SCRIPTURE STUDY

Every journey has two things in common. Each has a starting point and a destination. The spiritual journey is no different. The starting point of the spiritual journey is the call to discipleship. This call contains both a promise and an invitation. Its promise is grace and forgiveness to all who place their trust in Jesus Christ. Its invitation is to enlist in Christ's service. Those who receive the promise also bind themselves to

Christ's service and embark on a lifelong journey. Along the way, however, additional invitations are given to follow Christ in special service.

Read Luke 5:1–11 and John 1:40–42. Then answer the following questions.

What was Peter doing when Jesus promised to make him a "fisher of men"? _____

_____

_____

Was this the first time that Peter had met Jesus? _____

_____

_____

How did Peter initially respond to Jesus' invitation, according to Luke 5:5? Do you think he was exaggerating? _____

_____

_____

How did Jesus answer Peter's objection? _____

_____

_____

Theologians speak of several different kinds of "calling" in the Christian life. One form is the call to believe in Christ as Lord and Savior that is issued by the Holy Spirit working in concert with the preaching of the gospel. There is the separation to specialized service, usually thought of as "a call to the ministry." Then there is the special purpose that God has for each person in his or her own ordinary sphere of life, also described in Scripture as a calling.

Which of these kinds of callings is reflected in the following passages?

Matthew 11:28–30 _____

_____

Luke 5:27–32 _____

_____

Luke 9:57–62 _____

_____

Acts 13:1–3 _____

_____

1 Corinthians 7:21–23 _____

_____

According to the following Scripture passages, to what have those who are in Christ been called?

1 Corinthians 1:9 _____

_____

Colossians 3:15 _____

_____

1 Thessalonians 4:7 _____

_____

1 Timothy 6:12 _____

_____

1 Peter 5:10 _____

_____

I am astonished that you are so quickly deserting the one who called you by the grace of Christ and are turning to a different gospel. (Galatians 1:6)

He called you to this through our gospel, that you might share in the glory of our Lord Jesus Christ. (2 Thessalonians 2:14)

His divine power has given us everything we need for life and godliness through our knowledge of him who called us by his own glory and goodness. (2 Peter 1:3)

According to the above three verses, how did God call us? _____

_____

_____

God is the ultimate source of the calling we have received in Christ. However, He often uses human instruments to issue the call to follow Christ. How did God's servants play a critical role in calling others either to follow Jesus or to serve Him in the following passages?

Acts 9:1–19 _____

_____

Acts 13:1–5 _____

_____

Romans 10:11–15 _____

_____

All this is from God, who reconciled us to himself through Christ and gave us the ministry of reconciliation: that God was reconciling the world to himself in Christ, not counting men's sins against them. And he has committed to us the message of reconciliation. We are therefore Christ's ambassadors, as though God were making his appeal through us. We implore you on Christ's behalf: Be reconciled to God. (2 Corinthians 5:18–20)

What analogy does Paul use to describe his calling? _____
_____
_____

How does this help you to understand your own calling in Christ? _____
_____
_____

But when God, who set me apart from birth and called me by his grace, was pleased to reveal his Son in me so that I might preach him among the Gentiles, I did not consult any man, nor did I go up to Jerusalem to see those who were apostles before I was, but I went immediately into Arabia and later returned to Damascus. (Galatians 1:15–17)

What role did timing play in Paul's experience of God's calling in his life? _____
_____
_____

MY RESPONSE

1. How would you describe your own personal experience of God's call? _____
_____
_____

2. How have you responded to it? _____
_____
_____

3. Has God called you to serve Him in some special way? _____
_____
_____

4. Write a personal mission statement that reflects your understanding of God's calling and your gifts and abilities. _____
_____
_____

CONCLUSION

The call to receive Christ leads to other invitations. It is a call to follow after Him in obedience and to serve Him in His cause. Just as Peter was called first to be a disciple and then later called to serve as an apostle, some of us will experience a "special" calling to some particular ministry. However, all who follow Christ have been called to serve Him in whatever vocation they find themselves. Every Christian has been given spiritual gifts and has been charged with the responsibility of being a steward "of the manifold grace of God" (1 Peter 4:10 NASB).

PRAYER

Thank God for the way He has worked to make you aware of His purpose for your life. Ask Him to help you to be sensitive to His direction as you continue to respond to His call.

l e s s o n   t w o

STAGES OF COMMITMENT

KEY PASSAGE: *In all my prayers for all of you, I always pray with joy because of your partnership in the gospel from the first day until now, being confident of this, that he who began a good work in you will carry it on to completion until the day of Christ Jesus.*
(Philippians 1:4–6)

WISE WORDS

Think about people who find themselves in religious ruts. They discover a number of things about themselves. They will find that they are getting older but not getting any holier. Time is their enemy, not their friend. The time they trusted and looked to is betraying them, for they often said to themselves, "The passing of time will help me. I know some good old saints, so as I get older I'll get holier and better. Time will help me, purify me and revive me." They said that the year before last, but they were not helped any last year. Time betrayed them.

A. W. TOZER

So many times, you can't see anything happening week to week. Spiritual growth takes place beneath the surface.
STUART BRISCOE

THOUGHT STARTER

How many stages do you think there are in a person's physical growth? _____

_____

_____

In what way are there stages in the spiritual life? _____

_____

_____

Are some stages easier than others? Explain. _____

_____

_____

SCRIPTURE STUDY

Spiritual growth, like physical growth, occurs in stages. We are not suddenly transformed into a spiritually mature disciple when we are born again. We begin as a spiritual babe and must go through a process of spiritual development. This was the pattern reflected in the apostle Peter's spiritual life. What major spiritual development in Peter's spiritual progress is reflected in each of the passages below? (The passages are arranged in likely chronological order.)

John 1:41–42 _____

_____

Matthew 4:18–20 _____

_____

Luke 5:1–11 _____

_____

Matthew 14:25–33 _____

_____

Matthew 15:10–20 _____

_____

John 6:60–68 _____

_____

Mark 14:27–32 _____

_____

Luke 22:54–71 _____

_____

John 21:1–19 _____

_____

Acts 2:14–16 _____

_____

Galatians 2:11–21 _____

_____

Using the verses above, draw a graph of Peter's spiritual journey to show high and low points.

Which does God seem to have used more in Peter's life to further his spiritual development: success or failure?

_____

_____

How did Jesus use Peter's failures to help him be a more effective disciple? _____

_____

_____

MY RESPONSE

1. Draw a map below charting your own spiritual journey. Note the major "landmarks" that reflect significant spiritual developments along the way.

2. What parallels do you see between the stages of your spiritual journey and Peter's? _____

_____

_____

3. Can you identify a major lesson that you learned at each stage? _____ _____

_____

_____

CONCLUSION

The disciples we read about in the Bible were not superhuman. They were ordinary people who took God at His word and were used by Him in extraordinary ways. Unlike the scribes who were trained scholars, they were simply "laymen" who had spent time with Christ. Peter, in particular, was given to hasty judgments and rash commitments. He had a tendency to speak and act without thinking. Bold in his faith one minute, he sank beneath the waves of doubt and fear the next. Peter's character changed radically on the Day of Pentecost. Yet, even then, Peter still would have important lessons to learn. Like Peter, we never outgrow the learning process in the Christian life. Like him, we also often learn from our mistakes. As we progress through various stages of growth, there are always new graces to develop and new lessons to learn.

PRAYER

Read Psalm 139 and write your own prayer praising God for His guidance and asking Him to continue to lead you in the Christian life.

l e s s o n   t h r e e

BUMPS
IN THE
ROAD

KEY PASSAGE: *"Simon, Simon, Satan has asked to sift you as wheat. But I have prayed for you, Simon, that your faith may not fail. And when you have turned back, strengthen your brothers."* (Luke 22:31–32)

WISE WORDS

Fall seven times, stand up eight.

JAPANESE PROVERB

Often the doorway to success is entered through the hallway of failure.

ERWIN W. LUTZER

THOUGHT STARTER

Can you think of a time when you benefited from failure? _____

_____

_____

When is failure a bad thing? _____

_____

_____

When is it constructive? _____

_____

_____

SCRIPTURE STUDY

We tend to think of the successful Christian life as one that is marked by an unbroken string of successes. We believe that a truly "spiritual" person is one who "does it right the first time." Yet when we study the pattern of Christ's disciples we discover that more often than not their growth came through mistakes and failure. Their example is a reminder that the spiritual journey is not always a smooth one. There are often "bumps" along the way.

That day when evening came, he said to his disciples, "Let us go over to the other side." Leaving the crowd behind, they took him along, just as he was, in the boat. There were also other boats with him. A furious squall came up, and the

BUMPS IN THE ROAD   207

waves broke over the boat, so that it was nearly swamped. Jesus was in the stern, sleeping on a cushion. The disciples woke him and said to him, "Teacher, don't you care if we drown?" He got up, rebuked the wind and said to the waves, "Quiet! Be still!" Then the wind died down and it was completely calm. He said to his disciples, "Why are you so afraid? Do you still have no faith?" They were terrified and asked each other, "Who is this? Even the wind and the waves obey him!" (Mark 4:35–41)

Why were the disciples so alarmed? _____
_____
_____

Do you think their fear was reasonable or unreasonable (cf. Luke 8:23)? _____
_____
_____

What, according to Jesus, was the reason for their failure on this occasion? _____
_____
_____

What insight about Jesus did they learn as a result of this incident? _____
_____
_____

The fact that several of Christ's disciples were experienced fishermen suggests that, on a purely human level at least, their fears were reasonable. This storm was so bad that the boat was filling up with water, and the disciples were in real physical danger. Their root problem, which was a lack of faith, was reflected in their frantic question: "Teacher, don't you care if we drown?" They were filled with anxiety not because they overestimated the danger of the storm but because they had underestimated Christ's concern for them and His ability to deal with the problem.

Read the account of another time when Jesus helped his disciples learn through their misunderstanding. Read Mark 8:14–21, and then answer the following questions.

The disciples misunderstood Jesus' statement about the "yeast" of the Pharisees and of Herod. What was Jesus really talking about? What did the disciples think Jesus was talking about? _____
_____
_____

Why do you think they made this mistake? _____
_____
_____

What had the disciples failed to learn from the two incidents Jesus mentions in this passage? _____

_____

_____

Christ's disciples learned two important lessons as a result of this error. What were they? _____

_____

_____

The disciples' guilt over forgetting to bring bread for their journey caused them to misunderstand Jesus' statement. In addition, they had failed to learn from the two instances in which Christ had miraculously provided bread for the multitude. As a result, the lesson was twofold. Christ had intended His words to be a warning against the danger of hypocrisy. Their error transformed the occasion into a lesson about divine provision.

People were bringing little children to Jesus to have him touch them, but the disciples rebuked them. When Jesus saw this, he was indignant. He said to them, "Let the little children come to me, and do not hinder them, for the kingdom of God belongs to such as these. I tell you the truth, anyone who will not receive the kingdom of God like a little child will never enter it." And he took the children in his arms, put his hands on them and blessed them. (Mark 10:13–16)

Why were the people bringing children to Jesus? What did they want Him to do for them? _____

_____

_____

What did the disciples do? Why do you think they reacted this way? _____

_____

_____

How did Jesus respond when He learned that the disciples were rebuking these parents? What did He say to them? _____

_____

_____

What important lesson about Jesus did the disciples learn as a result of this? What did they learn about themselves? _____

_____

_____

It is likely that the disciples meant to spare Jesus trouble when they rebuked these parents. Perhaps they thought that He was too busy to be bothered by the seemingly insignificant task of pronouncing a blessing upon these children. As a result of Jesus' rebuke, the disciples learned that Jesus is deeply concerned about even the least significant person. They also learned something about Jesus' expectation for them when He used these children as a model of faith and humility.

Read Luke 9:46–50 about an argument among the disciples and Jesus' response. Then answer the following questions.

Why were the disciples arguing with one another? _____

_____

_____

How did Jesus know what they were discussing? _____

_____

_____

Why did the disciples forbid the man spoken of in Luke 9:49, if he was driving out demons in Jesus' name? _____

_____

_____

How did Jesus respond to John's statement? _____

_____

_____

What misconception on the part of the disciples do these two incidents have in common? _____

_____

_____

Although the examples given above could be multiplied many times over, the root problems that caused them focus on two primary areas of failure. The first was the failure to fully comprehend Christ's power. The disciples repeatedly underestimated Christ's ability to work on their behalf. The second failure was related to the first. The disciples often overestimated their own importance and abilities.

MY RESPONSE

Describe three occasions when you experienced failure, summarize the spiritual lessons you learned as a result, and describe how you are implementing those lessons today.

	Nature of the Failure	Spiritual Lesson	Impact Today
1.			
2.			
3.			

CONCLUSION

Failure is one of God's most common teaching tools. It shows us our need for God's grace and teaches us to depend upon Christ for growth and service. Failure leads to valuable knowledge about God and about ourselves. Through failure we discover our limitations and misperceptions, and through our recovery from failure we learn about God's power. As the Reformer Martin Luther observed, "It is the nature of God to make something out of nothing; therefore, when anyone is nothing, God may yet make something of him."

PRAYER

Think of a recent failure that you have experienced. Ask for God's insight so that you will benefit fully from the experience.

THE CONTEXT OF TRAINING: ENDURING HARDSHIP

KEY PASSAGE: *Endure hardship with us like a good soldier of Christ Jesus.*
(2 Timothy 2:3)

WISE WORDS

Meek endurance and meek obedience, the accepting of his dealings, of whatever complexion they are and however they may tear and desolate our hearts, without murmuring, without sulking, without rebellion or resistance, is the deepest conception of the meekness that Christ pronounced blessed.
ALEXANDER MACLAREN

Endurance is not just the ability to bear a hard thing, but to turn it into glory.
WILLIAM BARCLAY

THOUGHT STARTER

How would you define endurance? _____

_____

_____

Do you think of endurance as a positive or a negative quality? Why? _____

_____

_____

When is it most difficult to endure? _____

_____

_____

What makes endurance possible? _____

_____

_____

SCRIPTURE STUDY

Read Matthew 10:28–40. Then answer the following questions.

What challenges do those who follow Jesus face? _____

_____

_____

What warnings and promises does Jesus give to encourage them? _____

_____

_____

How does Jesus promise to help them? _____

_____

_____

Endure hardship with us like a good soldier of Christ Jesus. No one serving as a soldier gets involved in civilian affairs—he wants to please his commanding officer. Similarly, if anyone competes as an athlete, he does not receive the victor's crown unless he competes according to the rules. The hardworking farmer should be the first to receive a share of the crops. Reflect on what I am saying, for the Lord will give you insight into all this. (2 Timothy 2:3–7)

In these verses, Paul gives three examples from ordinary life where endurance is needed. In the box below, identify the three examples he gives. Explain why endurance is needed in each case and the benefit that comes as a result.

	The Example	Why Endurance Is Needed	The Benefit
1.			
2.			
3.			

In 2 Timothy 2:3–7 Paul gives three examples of situations where endurance is needed: the soldier, the athlete, and the farmer. The soldier endures because he or she is under the authority of a commander. Athletes endure for the sake of training and in order to win the competition. A farmer endures in the hope of reaping a harvest. In each case the one who endures is asked to conform to the expectations of someone or something else and does not have the liberty to do whatever he or she pleases. There is also a reward expected from each. For the soldier it is the satisfaction of pleasing the one in command. For the athlete it is the thrill of winning by the rules. For the hardworking farmer it is the reward of a harvest. Grace does not mean that Christian life is always easy. Endurance is an important discipline of the Christian life.

Read Romans 15:1–6. Then answer the following questions.

Why did the believers in Rome need endurance? You may want to read the entire chapter to understand the context of these verses. _____

_____

_____

Who did Paul use as an example of endurance? _____

_____

_____

How did Christ show endurance? _____

_____

_____

What has God provided to help us endure? _____

_____

_____

And we pray this in order that you may live a life worthy of the Lord and may please him in every way: bearing fruit in every good work, growing in the knowledge of God, being strengthened with all power according to his glorious might so that you may have great endurance and patience, and joyfully giving thanks to the Father, who has qualified you to share in the inheritance of the saints in the kingdom of light. (Colossians 1:10–12)

What preconditions to endurance does Paul mention in these verses? _____

_____

_____

Is the ability to endure purely a matter of the will? _____

_____

_____

What role does prayer play in our ability to endure? _____

_____

_____

Here is a trustworthy saying: If we died with him, we will also live with him; if we endure, we will also reign with him. If we disown him, he will also disown us; if we are faithless, he will remain faithful, for he cannot disown himself. (2 Timothy 2:11–13)

What warning does Paul give in these verses? _____
_____
_____

What encouragement does he provide? _____
_____
_____

Why do you think these promises would have motivated Timothy to endure hardship? _____
_____
_____

What kind of hardship was Paul experiencing when he wrote these words (cf. 2 Timothy 1:8; 4:6)? _____
_____
_____

Jesus is both an example of endurance and the source of endurance in the Christian life. He patiently endured insult and suffering in order to purchase the believer's redemption. He also promised a reward to those who endure on His behalf. When endurance is required of us, Jesus understands our struggle. He strengthens us so that we are able to endure the hardships that come with the Christian life and promises that those who endure will one day reign with Him.

MY RESPONSE

1. Where is endurance most needed in your life today? _____
_____
_____

2. What factors make it difficult for you to endure in this situation? _____
_____
_____

3. How can Christ's example motivate you to endure in this situation? _____
_____
_____

4. How can Christ's provision of power help you to endure? _____
_____
_____

5. Which of the passages from today's study could be used to encourage you to endure hardship in this difficult circumstance? _____

_____

_____

CONCLUSION

Trusting in Jesus Christ does not necessarily make life easier. In some respects, it makes life more difficult. Jesus warned His followers that becoming His disciple often leads to conflict within the family. The apostle Paul compared the life of discipleship to the rigors of military training or athletic competition. The opportunity to endure is also an opportunity to experience God's grace. God uses hardship and endurance to transform us into the image of Christ.

PRAYER

Ask God for the knowledge, motivation, and power that will help you to endure in the circumstance you identified above.

l e s s o n   f i v e

SPECIAL TRAINING:
THE VALUE OF
DIVINE DISCIPLINE

KEY PASSAGE: *Moreover, we have all had human fathers who disciplined us and we respected them for it. How much more should we submit to the Father of our spirits and live!*
(Hebrews 12:9)

WISE WORDS

If I ever had a problem, my parents never had a problem telling me I had a problem.
MICHAEL JORDAN

The fruit tree will not bear much fruit unless it is pruned and the useless branches cut away. The vine will not bear grapes unless it is pruned and the deadwood cut away. So it may be necessary for us to endure some pruning, some cutting away of deadwood, that we may bear good fruit.
ROBERT C. SHANNON

THOUGHT STARTER

Think of a time when your parents disciplined you. How did you feel about it at the time? _____

_____

_____

Do you feel the same way today? _____

_____

_____

What made your parents' perspective so different from your own? _____

_____

_____

Why do you view parental discipline differently today than when you experienced it as a child? _____

_____

_____

SCRIPTURE STUDY

God often uses hardship to help us grow. The author of Hebrews refers to this as "discipline" in Hebrews 12:7. However, this is a very special kind of discipline. In view of the "race" analogy of the previous verses, we might have expected him to use an athletic term. Instead, he uses a term that refers to parental training. When hardship enters our lives, it is often God's way of exercising parental discipline.

My son, do not despise the LORD's discipline and do not resent his rebuke, because the LORD disciplines those he loves, as a father the son he delights in. (Proverbs 3:11–12)

Consider him who endured such opposition from sinful men, so that you will not grow weary and lose heart. In your struggle against sin, you have not yet resisted to the point of shedding your blood. And you have forgotten that word of encouragement that addresses you as sons: "My son, do not make light of the Lord's discipline, and do not lose heart when he rebukes you, because the Lord disciplines those he loves, and he punishes everyone he accepts as a son." Endure hardship as discipline; God is treating you as sons. For what son is not disciplined by his father? If you are not disciplined (and everyone undergoes discipline), then you are illegitimate children and not true sons. (Hebrews 12:3–8)

What had those who first received the letter to the Hebrews forgotten? _____

_____

_____

How should they have interpreted the hardships they were currently facing? _____

_____

_____

The experience of divine discipline implies something important about those who experience it. What does divine discipline tell us about ourselves? _____

_____

_____

What does divine discipline tell us about God? _____

_____

_____

Moreover, we have all had human fathers who disciplined us and we respected them for it. How much more should we submit to the Father of our spirits and live! Our fathers disciplined us for a little while as they thought best; but God disciplines us for our good, that we may share in his holiness. No discipline seems pleasant at the time, but painful. Later on, however, it produces a harvest of righteousness and peace for those who have been trained by it. (Hebrews 12:9–11)

How is divine discipline like parental discipline? How does it differ? _____

_____

_____

What confidence can we have about divine discipline that we could not have about the discipline we received from our parents? _____

_____

_____

The writer of Hebrews describes a "before" and "after" picture of divine discipline. How does divine discipline seem when we are experiencing it? _____

_____

_____

How does it seem once it has done its work? What is the difference? _____

_____

_____

What is the end result of divine discipline? _____

_____

_____

Slaves, submit yourselves to your masters with all respect, not only to those who are good and considerate, but also to those who are harsh. For it is commendable if a man bears up under the pain of unjust suffering because he is conscious of God. But how is it to your credit if you receive a beating for doing wrong and endure it? But if you suffer for doing good and you endure it, this is commendable before God. . . . It is better, if it is God's will, to suffer for doing good than for doing evil. (1 Peter 2:18–20; 3:17)

Peter gives a good reason and a bad reason for suffering. When is it commendable to suffer? When is it not commendable? _____

_____

_____

MY RESPONSE

1. Are there any difficulties in your life that you now realize may be examples of divine discipline? _____

_____

_____

2. How should this knowledge change the way you respond to these circumstances? _____

_____

_____

3. What lessons do you think God wants you to learn as a result of this experience? _____

_____

_____

4. Are there changes that need to be made? _____

_____

_____

5. Have you received "a harvest of righteousness and peace" as a result of this experience? Explain your answer. _____

_____

_____

CONCLUSION

The secret to enduring divine discipline is to look at it through the eyes of God and interpret its message. Discipline tells us that God loves us enough to intervene in our lives—even to the point where it hurts. Divine discipline also tells us that God has accepted us as His children. The fact that He disciplines us indicates that we belong to Him. Although painful, once it has done its work divine discipline produces "a harvest of righteousness and peace" in those who submit to its training (Hebrews 12:11).

PRAYER

Thank God for His parental discipline. Ask Him to give you insight into the lessons He has for you in your present circumstances.

u n i t   t e n

THE NEW TESTAMENT MODEL OF DISCIPLESHIP

THE
GOAL OF
DISCIPLESHIP

KEY PASSAGE: *I have set you an example that you should do as I have done for you. I tell you the truth, no servant is greater than his master, nor is a messenger greater than the one who sent him.* (John 13:15–16)

WISE WORDS

Question 1: What is the chief end of man?
Answer: Man's chief end is to glorify God, and to enjoy him forever.
WESTMINSTER SHORTER CATECHISM

We must ask ourselves, Who am I trying to please? The worker endeavors to please his boss. The child his parents. The pupil his teacher. But for the believer, underpinning all that must be a heartfelt commitment to be able to say with Paul, "We make it our goal to please him" (2 Corinthians 5:9).
ALISTAIR BEGG

THOUGHT STARTER

What do you think it means to be a "disciple"? _____

_____

_____

What is the goal of the life of discipleship? _____

_____

_____

In what ways are you like Jesus? In what ways are you unlike Him? _____

_____

_____

SCRIPTURE STUDY

In the Bible college where I teach, I often ask my students how many of them want to be like Jesus. Invariably, every hand goes up. Their faces tell me that they think the question is an odd one. After all, what Christian doesn't want to be like Jesus? My next question, however, gets a very different response: "How many of you would say that you *are* like Jesus?" This time hardly a hand is raised. There are nervous chuckles throughout the room, as if to say, "Who in their right mind would make such a claim?"

I do not think that they are unusual. Experience has shown me that most believers would answer similarly. Yet is there not a fundamental contradiction in such a response? We are quick to say that we want to live like Jesus, but in reality we do not believe that it is possible. In effect, what we really mean is that we want to be "sort of" like Jesus. Christ may be our ideal, but He is not our model. Yet Jesus taught that at its heart biblical discipleship is the art of being apprenticed to Christ. He is both our ideal and our model. Our aim is to be like Him.

"A student is not above his teacher, nor a servant above his master. It is enough for the student to be like his teacher, and the servant like his master. If the head of the house has been called Beelzebub, how much more the members of his household!" (Matthew 10:24–25)

What, according to Jesus, is the disciple's primary objective? _____
_____
_____

Jesus' description of the discipleship process is a simple one. The goal of the student is to be like his master. Nothing more and nothing less. In saying this, He sets the agenda for His own disciples. They have been called to watch and imitate their master in all areas of life.

Jesus says that it is "enough" for the student to be like his teacher. What do you think Jesus would say about a disciple who was content to be less than his teacher? _____
_____
_____

When our lives resemble our master's, we will be treated like our master. This brings with it an inevitable implication. Those who love Christ will love those who are like Christ. Those who hate Christ will treat those who are like Christ the same way they have treated the Savior. There is a negative dimension to the life of discipleship.

Read John 13:12–17. Then answer the following questions.

How does Jesus describe His disciples' relationship to Him in these verses? _____
_____
_____

How does He expect them to respond? _____
_____
_____

In verse 17, Jesus promises a blessing if the servant does what? _____
_____
_____

The goal of the disciple in Jesus' day was to become a rabbi. He devoted himself to the study of Scripture and the memorization of the teaching handed down by the rabbi. Instruction was usually in the form of questions posed by the rabbi and answered by the student. Students addressed the rabbi as "master," "teacher," or sometimes "father," and they were expected to revere him more than their own parents.

Similarly, Jesus frequently used questions as a teaching device. And He warned His followers that anyone who did not love Him more than their own mother or father was not fit to be His disciple (Luke 14:26). He expected His disciples to remember His teaching and promised that the coming Holy Spirit would bring it to mind (John 14:23, 26). He expected His disciples to act upon His teaching and told them that the genuineness of their love for Him would be demonstrated by their obedience (John 14:23–24).

Be perfect, therefore, as your heavenly Father is perfect. (Matthew 5:48)

Be merciful, just as your Father is merciful. (Luke 6:36)

Who does Jesus say is our ultimate role model? _____

_____

_____

Read John 14:8–17. Then answer the following questions.

How do the Father, Son, and Holy Spirit work together to make this goal a reality in our lives? _____

_____

_____

What role does prayer play in this process? _____

_____

_____

Why will Jesus grant answers to our prayers? _____

_____

_____

MY RESPONSE

1. In what areas of your life do you feel that you are most like Jesus Christ? _____

_____

_____

2.In what areas of life are you least like Jesus Christ? _____

_____

_____

3. On the scale below, how would you rate your commitment to imitating Christ in your daily life?

Uncommitted   1   2   3   4   5   **Totally Committed**

4. Are you satisfied with how you have rated yourself? Why or Why not? _____

_____

_____

5. Jesus Christ is both the model and the means for attaining this high standard. We are not to "come up" to His level of behavior. The essence of discipleship is to allow Christ to live out His life in us. This is what Martin Luther meant when he said that we must first accept Christ as a gift before we can take Him as our example. What implication does this have for discipleship? _____

_____

_____

6. Have you received Jesus Christ as a gift by trusting in Him as your Savior and Lord? _____

_____

_____

CONCLUSION

Many view Christ's command to "be perfect . . . as your heavenly Father is perfect" as a worthy but unrealistic goal; we are so aware of our own sinfulness and weakness. Yet who is more aware of our sinfulness than the one who was made sin for us that "we might become the righteousness of God" (2 Corinthians 5:21)? The term that is translated "perfect" in Matthew 5:48 conveys the idea of that which is full or complete. In effect, Jesus' counsel is that we should "go all the way" in our striving for righteous behavior and not settle for less than the standard of God's own behavior. If we are unclear as to what that standard looks like in real life, we need only look to Jesus.

PRAYER

Write a prayer of response. Ask God to work in the areas of your life that need to be brought into conformity with the image of Christ. Be specific.

l e s s o n   t w o

THE
NATURE OF
DISCIPLESHIP

KEY PASSAGE: *I will not leave you as orphans; I will come to you. Before long, the world will not see me anymore, but you will see me. Because I live, you also will live.*
(John 14:18–19)

WISE WORDS

In going against the stream of the world's ways there are two biblical designations for people of faith that are extremely useful: disciple *and* pilgrim. *Disciple (*mathetes*) says we are people who spend our lives apprenticed to our master, Jesus Christ. We are in a growing-learning relationship, always. A disciple is a learner, but not in the academic setting of a schoolroom, rather at the work site of a craftsman. We do not acquire information about God but skills in faith.*

*Pilgrim (*parepidemos*) tells us we are people who spend our lives going someplace, going to God, and whose path for getting there is the way, Jesus Christ. We realize that "this world is not my home" and set out for the "Father's house." Abraham who "went out," is our archetype. . . . [Jesus] gives us directions: "I am the way, and the truth, and the life; no one comes to the Father but by me" (Jn. 14:5–6). . . . The letter to the Hebrews defines our program: . . . "Let us lay aside every weight, and sin which clings so closely, and let us run with perseverance the race that is set before us, looking to Jesus, the pioneer and perfecter of our faith." (Heb. 12:1–2).*
EUGENE PETERSON

THOUGHT STARTER

In what ways is the life of discipleship like an apprenticeship? _____

_____

_____

In what ways is it like a pilgrimage? _____

_____

_____

SCRIPTURE STUDY

What is the essence of discipleship? Is it primarily a matter of Bible reading and memorization of Scripture? Does it consist mostly of practicing spiritual disciplines like worship, fasting, or prayer? Certainly, these are important activities and will have a place in the spiritual life of those who follow Christ. Yet as important as they are, such things do not comprise the heart of discipleship.

Jesus went up on a mountainside and called to him those he wanted, and they came to him. He appointed twelve—designating them apostles —that they might be with him and that he might send them out to preach and to have authority to drive out demons. (Mark 3:13–15)

Who took the initiative in the calling of the Twelve? _____

_____

_____

What two purposes did Jesus have for those that He called? _____

_____

_____

Which goal is mentioned first? Why is this significant? _____

_____

_____

Jesus did not send out these disciples until Mark 6:7. What did they do until then? (Scan Mark 4 and 5 and read Mark 6:1–6 to determine their activities before He sent the Twelve on their journey.) _____

_____

_____

It is easy to see how the first disciples could "be with" Jesus. They traveled the roads of the Judean countryside with Him and ate with Him (Mark 2:23). They sat at His feet and listened to Him teach (Luke 10:39). They saw Him with their eyes and touched Him with their hands (1 John 1:1). Our experience is much different. We follow Christ but have never seen His face. We have never touched Him or heard His voice. Does this mean that we must be satisfied with less of a relationship?

The presence of the Holy Spirit in the disciple's life guarantees a level of intimacy that was unmatched even by those who walked with Jesus during His earthly ministry. Prior to His ascension, Jesus assured His disciples that He would come to them after His death and resurrection (John 14:18).

We do not need to see Jesus to be in relationship with Him. Indeed, Jesus promised a special blessing to those whose relationship with Him was based upon faith rather than sight (John 20:29). The early disciples were privileged to walk with Christ during His earthly ministry but only a select few had continual access to Him. Disciples today are privileged to have Christ dwelling in them through the ministry of the Holy Spirit. This is not a blessing reserved for an elite group within the church. It is the spiritual birthright of everyone who has trusted in Christ for eternal life.

You, however, are controlled not by the sinful nature but by the Spirit, if the Spirit of God lives in you. And if anyone does not have the Spirit of Christ, he does not belong to Christ. But if Christ is in you, your body is dead because of sin, yet your spirit is alive because of righteousness. And if the Spirit of him who raised Jesus from the dead is living in you, he who raised Christ from the dead will also give life to your mortal bodies through his Spirit, who lives in you. Therefore, brothers, we have an obligation—but it is not to the sinful nature, to live according to it. For if you live according to the sinful nature, you will die; but if by the Spirit you put to death the misdeeds of the body, you will live, because those who are led by the Spirit of God are sons of God. For you did not receive a spirit that makes you a slave again to fear, but you received the Spirit of sonship. And by him we cry, "Abba, Father." The Spirit himself testifies with our spirit that we are God's children. (Romans 8:9–16)

How can we be certain that we are indwelt by the Holy Spirit? _____

_____

_____

What practical help does the Holy Spirit provide in the life of discipleship? _____

_____

_____

What obligations do we have as those who have received the benefits of Christ's work and have a relationship with Him through the ministry of the Holy Spirit? _____

_____

_____

MY RESPONSE

1. Which do you think is most characteristic of your discipleship relationship with Jesus Christ, being with Him or doing things for Him? _____

_____

_____

2. What are the major barriers that are keeping you from deepening the "being" aspect of your relationship to Christ? _____

_____

_____

3. What barriers are hindering the "doing" side of this relationship? _____

_____

_____

4. How do you think that the ministry of the Holy Spirit might be able to help you remove these barriers? _____

_____

_____

CONCLUSION

At its core, true discipleship is first a matter of relationship rather than a series of tasks that must be accomplished. When this pattern is reversed, discipleship becomes drudgery. We may be doing the "right" things, but we do them for the wrong reason. The actions of a true disciple flow out of the disciple's relationship with Jesus Christ. Notice that when Jesus appointed the Twelve, His first goal for them was that they "might be with him" (Mark 3:14).

PRAYER

Focus on one of the barriers identified above and ask the Holy Spirit for wisdom and help in removing it.

l e s s o n   t h r e e

THE
DANGER OF
HYPOCRISY

KEY PASSAGE: *"For I tell you that unless your righteousness surpasses that of the Pharisees and the teachers of the law, you will certainly not enter the kingdom of heaven."*
(Matthew 5:20)

WISE WORDS

Hateful to me even as the gates of Hades is he that hideth one thing in his heart and uttereth another.

HOMER

"Woe to you, teachers of the law and Pharisees, you hypocrites! You give a tenth of your spices—mint, dill and cummin. But you have neglected the more important matters of the law—justice, mercy and faithfulness. You should have practiced the latter, without neglecting the former. You blind guides! You strain out a gnat but swallow a camel."

MATTHEW 23:23–24

THOUGHT STARTER

1. How would you define hypocrisy *in a single sentence?* _____

_____

_____

2. Why do you think Jesus condemned hypocrisy so strongly? _____

_____

_____

3. When are you the most tempted to act hypocritically? _____

_____

_____

SCRIPTURE STUDY

Read Matthew 6:1–6, from Jesus' Sermon on the Mount. Then answer the following questions.

Jesus criticized the religious leaders of His day. What did He say motivated them in their religious practices?

_____

_____

_____

Why did He label this as "hypocrisy"? _____

_____

_____

How does Jesus compare and contrast these religious leaders with those who would be His disciples in Matthew 23:1–12? Use the table below to chart your answers.

Teachers of the Law and Pharisees	The Disciples of Jesus
_____	_____
_____	_____
_____	_____

What traits of the teachers of the Law and the Pharisees does Jesus condemn? _____

_____

_____

How would you summarize the major difference between true discipleship and religious hypocrisy based upon Jesus' words? _____

_____

_____

MY RESPONSE

1. What evidence of spiritual hypocrisy do you currently see in your own life? Be specific. _____

_____

_____

2. Where would you most like to see change in your life at this time? What steps do you need to take to make this a reality? _____

_____

_____

CONCLUSION

Jesus condemned the teachers of the Law and the Pharisees because they were more concerned about the way they appeared to others than they were about God. They seemed to be deeply concerned about obeying God's Law, when in reality they were more interested in finding loopholes. True disciples are not afraid of allowing their acts of righteousness to be seen, but that is not their primary aim in obeying Christ.

PRAYER

Write a brief prayer asking God to increase your fruitfulness in the area described above. Ask for His help to take necessary steps that you have outlined in your answer.

THE
IMPORTANCE OF
COMMITMENT

KEY PASSAGE: *Jesus replied, "No one who puts his hand to the plow and looks back is fit for service in the kingdom of God."*
(Luke 9:62)

WISE WORDS

Then said Evangelist, "Keep that light in your eye, and go up directly thereto, so shalt thou see the gate; at which when thou knockest, it shall be told thee what thou shalt do." So I saw in my dream that the man began to run. Now he had not run far from his own door when his wife and children perceiving it, began to cry after him to return; but the man put his fingers in his ears and ran on, crying, "Life! life! eternal life!"
JOHN BUNYAN

THOUGHT STARTER

If you were asked to name the three most committed people you know, who would be on your list and why?

_____

_____

_____

How do these people differ from others? _____

_____

_____

What do you think is the secret to their commitment? _____

_____

_____

SCRIPTURE STUDY

Although the New Testament usually uses the term *disciple* to refer to those who were fully committed to Jesus Christ, sometimes the term is used to speak of those whose commitment was questionable. (See, for example, Matthew 8:18–22.) In such cases, the term *disciple* probably refers to only to those who followed Jesus' ministry but were not genuinely committed to Him.

In a few instances the New Testament even uses the term *disciple* to refer to those who later abandoned Jesus Christ (John 6:66). The most striking example of this is the case of Judas (Matthew 10:1; 11:1; 20:17). Although Judas was numbered among the disciples, it is clear that he was never a true believer. Jesus even referred to him as a "devil" (John 6:70; cf. 6:64).

As they were walking along the road, a man said to him, "I will follow you wherever you go." Jesus replied, "Foxes have holes and birds of the air have nests, but the Son of Man has no place to lay his head." He said to another man, "Follow me." But the man replied, "Lord, first let me go and bury my father." Jesus said to him, "Let the dead bury their own dead, but you go and proclaim the kingdom of God." Still another said, "I will follow you, Lord; but first let me go back and say good-by to my family." Jesus replied, "No one who puts his hand to the plow and looks back is fit for service in the kingdom of God." (Luke 9:57–62)

What point do you think Jesus was trying to make when He said, "Foxes have holes and birds of the air have nests, but the Son of Man has no place to lay his head"? What was it about the man's statement that prompted Jesus to say this? _____

_____

_____

What concern did the second man have? Was this an unreasonable request? _____

_____

_____

Why do you think Jesus responds to him in this way? What does Jesus' response imply about those who are not Christ's disciples? _____

_____

_____

What was wrong with the third man's offer to follow Jesus? Why do you think Jesus regarded this as "looking back"? _____

_____

_____

Read Mark 10:17–31. Then answer the following questions.

How did the young man in these verses approach Jesus? Do you think he was sincere? Why or why not? _____

_____

_____

How does Jesus respond to his question? Why is this surprising (Galatians 2:16)? _____

_____

_____

Ultimately, what was this man lacking? What was keeping him from doing what Jesus asked? _____

_____

_____

What did Jesus say was the solution to his problem in vv. 26–27? _____

_____

_____

How does Peter respond to this incident? What do you think prompted Peter's remark? _____

_____

_____

Did Jesus disagree with Peter's statement? _____

_____

_____

Jesus promises three things to those who have forsaken all to follow Him. What are they? _____

_____

_____

When do the blessings that come from following Jesus begin? In what do they culminate? _____

_____

_____

MY RESPONSE

1. Which of the individuals in the passages above do you identify with most? Why? _____

_____

_____

2. Have you struggled in the past in your commitment to Jesus? In what areas? How did you overcome these struggles? _____

_____

_____

3. Where do you feel you are strongest in your commitment to Jesus? Where do you feel you are weakest? _____

_____

_____

4. Jesus warned His disciples that those who followed Him would be called upon to make sacrifices. Yet He also promised that the blessings that come with discipleship would outweigh the sacrifices. List some of the areas in your life where you have experienced the kind of blessings Jesus describes in Mark 10:28–31. _____

_____

_____

CONCLUSION

There is an important dimension of Spirit-empowered human responsibility in the discipleship relationship. Grace and obedience are not at odds with one another in the Gospel. Both aspects of the salvation experience are emphasized by the apostle in 2 Timothy 2:19: "Nevertheless, God's solid foundation stands firm, sealed with this inscription: 'The Lord knows those who are his,' and, 'Everyone who confesses the name of the Lord must turn away from wickedness.'"

PRAYER

Write a brief prayer that thanks God for each of the blessings you identified in the previous question. Ask Him for His help in the area where you struggle most in your commitment to Jesus. _____

_____

_____

_____

_____

l e s s o n   f i v e

THE PORTRAIT
OF A
DISCIPLE

KEY PASSAGE: *When the disciples saw him walking on the lake, they were terrified. "It's a ghost," they said, and cried out in fear. But Jesus immediately said to them: "Take courage! It is I. Don't be afraid." "Lord, if it's you," Peter replied, "tell me to come to you on the water." "Come," he said. Then Peter got down out of the boat, walked on the water and came toward Jesus. But when he saw the wind, he was afraid.*
(Matthew 14:26–30)

WISE WORDS

By that which is spoken of him in diverse passages of the Gospel, he is very remarkable among the Apostles, both for his graces, and his failings; eminent in zeal and courage, and yet stumbling oft in his forwardness, and once grossly falling.

ROBERT LEIGHTON

THOUGHT STARTER

What comes first to your mind when you think of Peter—his successes or his failures? _____

_____

_____

Which do you think had the greatest impact on his life? _____

_____

_____

SCRIPTURE STUDY

Read Luke 5:1–8. Then answer the following questions.

These verses describe Peter's "call" to discipleship. What was Peter doing when Jesus called him? How did he respond? _____

_____

_____

What do you think it was about this incident that made Peter so aware of his own sinfulness? _____

_____

_____

John 1:41–42 seems to indicate that Peter was already aware of Jesus' ministry when this took place. To what, then, was Jesus calling Peter? _____

_____

_____

Read the following passages: Matthew 14:23–31; 16:21–23; Mark 10:25–31; 14:29–31; John 13:1–9; 18:1–11.

What impression of Peter's personality do you get from these passages? _____

_____

_____

What were his strengths? _____

_____

_____

What were his weaknesses? _____

_____

_____

While the salvation experience radically changes the believer's nature and character, it does not fundamentally alter a Christian's personality. Someone who was shy prior to his or her salvation experience does not suddenly become a "people person" after making a commitment to Christ. Those who are outgoing continue to be outgoing. If I hated opera before becoming a Christian, I will probably continue to hate opera. God has taken all of this into account. He has planned to incorporate my strengths into His calling for my life and is able to glorify Himself through me despite my weaknesses.

"Simon, Simon, Satan has asked to sift you as wheat. But I have prayed for you, Simon, that your faith may not fail. And when you have turned back, strengthen your brothers." (Luke 22:31–32)

On the night of His arrest, Jesus warned Peter that Satan desired to "sift him as wheat." What step did Jesus take to protect Peter? _____

_____

_____

Did Jesus expect Peter to successfully avoid the temptation that was coming his way? What does this suggest about Jesus' use of failure in the training of a disciple? _____

_____

_____

Compare Peter's behavior in Luke 22:54–61 with his behavior in Acts 2:12–24. How do you explain the difference? _____

_____

_____

What role does the Holy Spirit play in the discipleship experience (cf. Galatians 5:1–25)? _____

_____

_____

Peter was not immune to failure even after he had been a disciple for several years. In Galatians 2:11–14 the apostle Paul describes an occasion when he was forced to rebuke Peter publicly because of his hypocritical behavior toward the Gentiles. What prompted Peter to behave this way? _____

_____

_____

What does this imply about the place of accountability in the life of a disciple? _____

_____

_____

MY RESPONSE

Identify two important successes and two major failures you have experienced as a follower of Jesus. Identify the key lessons learned from each.

	Successes	Lessons Learned	Failures	Lessons Learned
1.	_____	_____	_____	_____
	_____	_____	_____	_____
2.	_____	_____	_____	_____
	_____	_____	_____	_____

CONCLUSION

Jesus saw something in Peter that this future apostle could not see in himself. Jesus foresaw the transformation that he would experience as a result of his commitment to Christ. Failure was one of the most common tools used by Jesus to shape Peter into the "fisher of men" that he was destined to become. Successful discipleship is not marked by the absence of failure so much as it is by the presence of grace in the midst of failure.

PRAYER

Thank God for the way He has designed your personality. Identify at least three strengths and one weakness, and ask Him to use them for His glory.

THE
LEARNER AS
TEACHER

LAYING
THE
FOUNDATION

KEY PASSAGE: *But as for you, continue in what you have learned and have become convinced of, because you know those from whom you learned it, and how from infancy you have known the holy Scriptures, which are able to make you wise for salvation through faith in Christ Jesus.*
(2 Timothy 3:14–15)

WISE WORDS

The Word is very plain, "Teach them diligently"; and if we want them to grow up a blessing to the Church of God and to the world, we must teach them.
D. L. MOODY

We take care of our possessions for our children. But of the children themselves we take no care at all. What an absurdity is this! Form the soul of thy son aright, and all the rest will be added hereafter.
JOHN CHRYSOSTOM

THOUGHT STARTER

What advantages do you see to receiving spiritual training as a child? _____
_____
_____

What pitfalls can occur in such training? How might they be avoided? _____
_____
_____

Do you know someone who was discipled in the home? How did this experience affect that person? _____
_____
_____

SCRIPTURE STUDY

We often think of discipleship as something that takes place in the church. While this is an important aspect of the discipleship experience, ideally the foundational lessons of discipleship are first learned in the home.

Children, obey your parents in the Lord, for this is right. "Honor your father and mother"—which is the first commandment with a promise—"that it may go well with you and that you may enjoy long life on the earth." Fathers, do not exasperate your children; instead, bring them up in the training and instruction of the Lord. (Ephesians 6:1–4)

Any kind of training has a positive and a negative dimension. What is the positive dimension? _____

_____

_____

What is the negative aspect of training? _____

_____

_____

Why are they both important? _____

_____

_____

The positive aspect of training involves instruction. The negative dimension involves correction. Both are essential. Instruction tells us what to do and shows us how. Correction points out the things that we need to change. Each dimension complements the other.

Hear, O Israel: The LORD our God, the LORD is one. Love the LORD your God with all your heart and with all your soul and with all your strength. These commandments that I give you today are to be upon your hearts. Impress them on your children. Talk about them when you sit at home and when you walk along the road, when you lie down and when you get up. (Deuteronomy 6:4–7)

Where did Moses envision that foundational training in God's Law would take place? _____

_____

_____

Does this seem like formal or informal instruction? _____

_____

_____

Who was the primary object of this training? _____

_____

_____

What kinds of "visual aids" were to be used in this training? _____

_____

_____

What other methods of instruction are reflected in the following passages from the Old Testament?

Leviticus 10:8–11 _____

_____

Deuteronomy 4:9 _____

_____

Deuteronomy 6:20 _____

_____

Deuteronomy 11:19 _____

_____

Deuteronomy 31:11–13 _____

_____

Deuteronomy 32:44–47 _____

_____

Spiritual training in the home during the Old Testament era involved a variety of teaching methods. One important way parents communicated spiritual truth was through storytelling. Israelite parents who had experienced God's deliverance were commanded to teach them to their children and their grandchildren (Deuteronomy 4:9). Parents were to talk repeatedly with their children about God's commandments as they went about their daily routine (6:7–9; 11:19). This instruction, however, was not one-sided. Children often asked questions about the meaning of the stipulations, decrees, and laws that Israel was required to observe (6:20). Public worship was also an important instructional tool (31:11–13; cf. Nehemiah 8:2–3). Every day was an opportunity to teach and every situation a classroom.

Read what 2 Timothy 1:5; 3:14–15 and Philippians 2:19–22 say about Timothy's spiritual background. Then answer the following questions.

How young was Timothy when his spiritual training began? _____

_____

_____

What was primarily used to train him? _____

_____

_____

Who was involved in the training process? _____

_____

_____

What impact did this combined effort in discipleship have on Timothy? _____

_____

_____

Read Psalm 139. What encouragement does this psalm offer to those who did not have the advantage of growing up in a Christian home? _____

_____

_____

Timothy had the advantage of being taught the Scriptures "from infancy," but many of us come from homes with parents who were not believers. In the case of those who have unbelieving parents, God works through the providential ordering of our lives, often teaching us lessons that are difficult to see at the time. Significant spiritual input may not come until later in life. Whether or not you have had the advantage of being taught the Scriptures from infancy, you can be confident that God's perfect timing and His providential ordering of your life have laid a valuable foundation for your spiritual life and ministry. And even without a parent's spiritual input, you can study the "Scriptures, which are able to make you wise" (2 Timothy 3:15).

MY RESPONSE

1. Identify three important lessons you learned as a result of your family background and explain how they shape your Christian life today.

a. _____

_____

_____

b. _____

_____

_____

c. _____

_____

_____

2. What evidence do you see of God's providence in ordering your family background in order to draw you to Himself? _____

_____

_____

CONCLUSION

Our family background and life experiences, no matter how unlikely, were not accidental. They are all part of God's larger plan. This was how the apostle Paul viewed his own personal history. He did not believe that God's purpose for his life began only when he trusted in Christ. He had been raised in Judaism and was once a persecutor of the church. Yet when the time was right, God, who had set Paul apart for the gospel from birth, revealed Christ to him and called him to apostolic ministry (Galatians 1:13–16). Whether directly or indirectly, formally or informally, those who have come to know Christ have been going through a training process that began in childhood.

PRAYER

Ask God to help you see more clearly how He has used your family background to shape you. If you are a parent, ask for His wisdom and help in discipling your children.

DISCIPLESHIP THROUGH MENTORING

KEY PASSAGE: *Join with others in following my example, brothers, and take note of those who live according to the pattern we gave you.*
(Philippians 3:17)

WISE WORDS

What ultimately determines the effectiveness of the mentoring process is not a person's style or skills or temperament, but a person's character, commitment, and love.

RON LEE DAVIS

Evidence mounts: most of what I experience and have experienced in the way of help, encouragement, and wisdom in the actual day-by-day believing and praying, loving and hoping, helping and persevering, obeying and sacrificing in the name and for the sake of Jesus comes from people who aren't considered competent to give it.

EUGENE PETERSON

THOUGHT STARTER

Who, besides your parents, have had a significant impact on your spiritual life? _____

_____

_____

What did they do to make such an impact on you? _____

_____

_____

How much of this experience occurred through formal training? _____

_____

_____

How much of it was informal? _____

_____

_____

SCRIPTURE STUDY

Paul attested to the value of family-based training when he said that he had no other colleague like Timothy, who cared more for the interests of Christ than for his own (Philippians 2:20). But parental instruction was not the only influence in Timothy's life. God also used Paul as a spiritual mentor to refine the lessons Timothy had learned at home. Timothy became Paul's spiritual apprentice and was trained by him in ministry.

But you know that Timothy has proved himself, because as a son with his father he has served with me in the work of the gospel. (Philippians 2:22)

To Timothy my true son in the faith: Grace, mercy and peace from God the Father and Christ Jesus our Lord. (1 Timothy 1:2)

To Timothy, my dear son: Grace, mercy and peace from God the Father and Christ Jesus our Lord. (2 Timothy 1:2)

According to these verses, how did Paul and Timothy view their relationship? _____

_____

_____

Why would this be an important perspective in a mentoring relationship? _____

_____

_____

How does Paul describe Timothy in the following passages?

Romans 16:21 _____

_____

1 Corinthians 4:17 _____

_____

2 Corinthians 1:1 _____

_____

Philippians 1:1 _____

_____

Don't let anyone look down on you because you are young, but set an example for the believers in speech, in life, in love, in faith and in purity. (1 Timothy 4:12)

For this reason I remind you to fan into flame the gift of God, which is in you through the laying on of my hands. For God did not give us a spirit of timidity, but a spirit of power, of love and of self-discipline. (2 Timothy 1:6–7)

Paul knew Timothy well enough to be aware of his weaknesses as well as his strengths. What weakness did Paul address in the two passages above? _____

_____

_____

How did Paul encourage Timothy? _____

_____

_____

Timothy served a kind of spiritual apprenticeship with Paul. He traveled with him on his missionary journeys and often acted as his representative (Acts 16:1–4; 19:22). Paul, in turn, served as Timothy's role model. So much so, in fact, that when Paul wanted the Corinthians to imitate his behavior he sent Timothy to remind them of his way of life. In his epistles Paul describes Timothy as a "fellow worker," a "son," a "brother," and a "servant." Paul felt a deep affection for Timothy, referring to him as his "true" and "dear" son. He was aware of Timothy's weaknesses and prayed for him regularly.

Likewise, teach the older women to be reverent in the way they live, not to be slanderers or addicted to much wine, but to teach what is good. Then they can train the younger women to love their husbands and children, to be self-controlled and pure, to be busy at home, to be kind, and to be subject to their husbands, so that no one will malign the word of God. (Titus 2:3–5)

Why might the relationship between older and younger women described in these verses be characterized as a "mentoring" relationship? _____

_____

_____

In what context does this mentoring ordinarily seem to have taken place? _____

_____

_____

Mentoring was not unique to Paul and Timothy. In Titus 2:3–5 Paul tells older women to be reverent in their behavior so that they can "train the younger women to love their husbands and children, to be self-controlled and pure, to be busy at home, to be kind, and to be subject to their husbands, so that no one will malign the word of God." This kind of training involved informal modeling through behavior. It did not take place in a classroom but in the context of daily living. It probably did not involve a scheduled time for teaching or a formal curriculum because its lessons were more "caught" than "taught."

Read Acts 18:24–28. Then answer the following questions.

What did Priscilla and Aquila do for Apollos? _____

_____

_____

Do you think this was a "formal" discipleship relationship? _____

_____

_____

How did it impact Apollos's ministry? _____

_____

_____

MY RESPONSE

1. Make a list of the mentors who have contributed to your spiritual development. _____

_____

_____

2. How is God using you to shape the spiritual lives of others? _____

_____

_____

3. While you may not think of yourself as a mentor, can you identify at least one other person for whom you act as a model? _____

_____

_____

CONCLUSION

In simplest terms, mentoring is modeling. The mentor acts as a living example of the Christian life for the one being discipled. While it may sometimes occur within the context of a formal setting, most of the training that takes place in a mentoring relationship is informal. There are no lesson plans. There is no classroom or lecture. Like Christ's disciples, those who are being mentored are "with" the one doing the discipling.

PRAYER

Pray for those you have identified as your spiritual mentors. Thank God for them, and ask Him to use them in the lives of others. Pray for those who look to you as an example of the Christian life.

QUALITIES OF A DISCIPLE MAKER: PART 1

KEY PASSAGE: *You, however, know all about my teaching, my way of life, my purpose, faith, patience, love, endurance, persecutions, sufferings—what kinds of things happened to me in Antioch, Iconium and Lystra, the persecutions I endured. Yet the Lord rescued me from all of them.*
(2 Timothy 3:10–11)

WISE WORDS

Jesus' leadership development of his undershepherds was not so much a course or a curriculum as it was a shared life. It was an experience of fellowship.
LEIGHTON FORD

I can't remember him ever instructing me or giving me advice. There was no hint of condescension or authority. The faith was simply there, spoken and acted out in the midst of whatever else we were doing—shooting, rowing, retrieving; or at other times, working or worshiping or meeting on the street and making small talk.
EUGENE PETERSON

THOUGHT STARTER

What do you think is the most important quality in an effective disciple maker? _____

_____

_____

Is there a "disciple making" personality type or can anyone disciple others? _____

_____

_____

What are the four or five qualities of those that God has used to shape your spiritual life that enabled them to be effective? _____

_____

_____

SCRIPTURE STUDY

Effective disciple making begins with availability. It takes time to make disciples. This is implied in the statement of Mark 3:14, which says that Jesus "appointed twelve . . . that they might be with him." He spent extended periods of time with three of His disciples, Peter, James, and John. These three were later regarded as "pillars" in the early church (Galatians 2:9).

In what ways did Jesus spend extended periods of time with His three key disciples, according to the following passages?

Matthew 17:1 _____
_____

Mark 5:37 _____
_____

Mark 13:3–4 _____
_____

Mark 14:33 _____
_____

1 John 1:1 _____
_____

Jesus' training program for the disciples was not limited to a few hours a week. It was carried on seven days a week. The disciples traveled and ate with Jesus. They watched Him engage in public ministry and saw how He lived in private. In addition, Jesus often took Peter, James, and John aside for special instruction. The experience was so vivid that John would later summarize it in these words: "That which was from the beginning, which we have heard, which we have seen with our eyes, which we have looked at and our hands have touched" (1 John 1:1).

Read 2 Corinthians 6:3–13. Then answer the following questions.

In what kinds of circumstances did Paul serve as a model for others? _____
_____
_____

What was his attitude toward those he discipled? _____
_____
_____

What did he say was his ultimate desire? _____
_____
_____
_____
_____
_____

Read Acts 20:17–38. In this passage Paul describes the nature of his ministry at Ephesus. What does it reveal about his character, motives, methods, and concerns?

Verse	Character	Motives	Methods	Concerns
17–21	_____	_____	_____	_____
22–24	_____	_____	_____	_____
25–31	_____	_____	_____	_____
32–35	_____	_____	_____	_____
36–38	_____	_____	_____	_____

Disciple making is as much a matter of modeling as it is teaching. Since the disciple maker's life is the content of the curriculum, one of the most important characteristics of a disciple maker is transparency. Paul's approach to disciple making combined "plain speaking" with "plain living." Teaching was an important part of Paul's discipleship ministry; but the example of his life was equally important.

MY RESPONSE

1. Which of Paul's character traits, motives, methods, and concerns do you see reflected in your own life and ministry?

_____

_____

_____

2. Where are they most evident? _____

_____

_____

3. Which would you like to see developed to a greater degree? _____

_____

_____

4. What can you do to strengthen this area? _____

_____

_____

CONCLUSION

The biblical model of disciple making is not the eastern notion of an enlightened guru who has reached a state of perfection but of a fellow struggler who encourages others as they both experience the same growth process. Both the mentor and the one being mentored are on the same journey. The difference is that the mentor is a little further down the path.

PRAYER

Read through Paul's address to the Ephesians again and use it as the basis for your own prayer. Pray for yourself, asking God to develop the qualities you see reflected in Paul's words. Pray for those you are discipling.

QUALITIES OF A DISCIPLE MAKER: PART 2

KEY PASSAGE: *Stand firm then, with the belt of truth buckled around your waist, with the breastplate of righteousness in place, and with your feet fitted with the readiness that comes from the gospel of peace. In addition to all this, take up the shield of faith, with which you can extinguish all the flaming arrows of the evil one. Take the helmet of salvation and the sword of the Spirit, which is the word of God. And pray in the Spirit on all occasions with all kinds of prayers and requests. With this in mind, be alert and always keep on praying for all the saints.*
(Ephesians 6:14–18)

WISE WORDS

Be what you would have your pupils be.

THOMAS CARLYLE

The basics are simple. The Bible sees the Christian life as a pilgrimage that goes from "here" to "there" through an experience of sanctifying change.

HAROLD LONGENECKER

THOUGHT STARTER

Who was your favorite teacher in school? _____

_____

_____

Would you say that your favorite teacher was also your most effective teacher? _____

_____

_____

What was it about his or her teaching that you remember the most? _____

_____

_____

How did the instructor's character and personality contribute to his or her overall effectiveness? _____

_____

_____

SCRIPTURE STUDY

Disciple making is really the process of transformation by observing the truth lived out by another. Consequently, one of the most important qualities of an effective disciple maker is a commitment to the truth. The first item mentioned in Paul's list of the armor of faith in Ephesians 6:14–18 is the "belt of truth." The belt provided the soldier with support and held other important pieces of armor in place.

Unlike so many, we do not peddle the word of God for profit. On the contrary, in Christ we speak before God with sincerity, like men sent from God. . . . Therefore, since through God's mercy we have this ministry, we do not lose heart. Rather, we have renounced secret and shameful ways; we do not use deception, nor do we distort the word of God. On the contrary, by setting forth the truth plainly we commend ourselves to every man's conscience in the sight of God. (2 Corinthians 2:17; 4:1–2)

Paul's ministry was driven by a commitment to the truth. This meant that there were some things he would not do. What were they? _____

_____

_____

Why might Paul have been tempted to tamper with God's truth? _____

_____

_____

In his appeal to the conscience of others, what did Paul present in addition to the truth? _____

_____

_____

How did Paul's sense of his own accountability to God affect his ministry to others in this area? _____

_____

_____

Paul's commitment to the truth was reflected in his willingness to speak the truth in love no matter what the cost. He was concerned about others and made every effort to gain a hearing. Yet he refused to manipulate others or water down the content of his teaching simply to gain a hearing. Although he was "seeker sensitive" in his approach to making disciples, he was not seeker driven. The fact that he saw himself as serving "in the sight of God" served as a safeguard against compromise and provided him with a constant reminder that he would eventually be accountable for both his motives and his methods.

Obey your leaders and submit to their authority. They keep watch over you as men who must give an account. Obey them so that their work will be a joy, not a burden, for that would be of no advantage to you. (Hebrews 13:17)

How does the writer of Hebrews describe the ministry of those who are characterized as "leaders" in this verse?

_____

_____

_____

The Greek term that is translated "keep watch" literally meant "to remain awake." What does the image of sleepless nights suggest about the nature of their ministry? _____

_____

_____

To whom must they one day give an account? For what? _____

_____

_____

In view of this, what kind of expectations should the disciple maker have of those who are being discipled? _____

_____

_____

Who does the writer of Hebrews say will be at a disadvantage if there is little or no progress? _____

_____

_____

Spiritual leaders must give an account to God, not only for their motives and methods in ministry, but also for the spiritual progress of those they have been called to serve. They are not accountable for how others respond to the truth but will one day be asked to evaluate the progress of those they have discipled. This implies that the disciple maker will have a standard of expectation of those who are being discipled.

Titus was discipled by Paul. Read Paul's descriptions of Titus in 2 Corinthians 8:16–17 and 12:14–19. What reflections of Paul's own values and character do you see in the ministry of Titus? _____

_____

_____

MY RESPONSE

1. Can you think of a time when you were tempted to downplay the truth when dealing with others? What made this tempting? How did you respond? _____

_____

_____

2. Whose image would others see reflected in your Christian life and ministry? Where would they see it? _____

_____

_____

3. If those who you have been used to disciple were to give an account to God for your spiritual development today, how would you feel about it? _____

_____

_____

4. What changes would you like to take place before such an account is given? _____

_____

_____

CONCLUSION

It is tempting to see training as primarily a matter of technique. The thinking is that if we use the right method, we will get the desired result. Knowing a variety of teaching methods is valuable; yet when it comes to discipleship, the character of the disciple maker is what is most important. The disciple maker's goal goes beyond simply trying to get others to do something. The objective, ultimately, is a Christ-centered way of life. As Thomas Carlyle observed, to make disciples, we must first be what we want those we disciple to be.

PRAYER

Spend some time reflecting on your own progress in the spiritual life and the progress of those you are discipling, and then write a prayer of response. _____

_____

_____

_____

_____

THE STEWARDSHIP OF DISCIPLE MAKING

KEY PASSAGE: *The Lord answered, "Who then is the faithful and wise manager, whom the master puts in charge of his servants to give them their food allowance at the proper time? It will be good for that servant whom the master finds doing so when he returns. I tell you the truth, he will put him in charge of all his possessions.* (Luke 12:42–44)

WISE WORDS

Our goal as mentors is not simply to make carbon copies of ourselves, but to spur others on to even greater things than we ourselves have achieved.

RON LEE DAVIS

If he is to carry out his trust fully, the leader will devote time to training others to succeed and perhaps even supersede him.

J. OSWALD SANDERS

THOUGHT STARTER

1. Have you ever trained someone to do something only to find that the person did it better than you? _____

_____

_____

2. How did it make you feel? _____

_____

_____

3. In what ways is discipling another person an investment? _____

_____

_____

SCRIPTURE STUDY

Disciple making is a form of stewardship. It is a stewardship of people. In the corporate realm, successful companies have recognized that their most valuable resources do not lie in the buildings or equipment that provide the infrastructure for what they do. As important as these things are, a company's most valuable asset is its people. A business that pays more attention to its buildings than it does to its people will be unsuccessful in the long run. If this is true of a business, it is doubly true of the church. Disciple making is a ministry of service. It is work that benefits others, and its primary goal is one of helping others to reach their full potential in Christ.

Read Luke 12:35–44. Then answer the following questions.

What command does Jesus give in verses 35–36? _____

_____

_____

How will the master respond to those servants who are found watching when He returns? _____

_____

_____

What responsibilities does the "faithful and wise manager" have, according to verse 42? _____

_____

_____

How does this parable help you to understand the biblical concept of stewardship? _____

_____

_____

What do you think would be the equivalent in the context of the church's ministry? _____

_____

_____

In the church at Antioch there were prophets and teachers: Barnabas, Simeon called Niger, Lucius of Cyrene, Manaen (who had been brought up with Herod the tetrarch) and Saul. While they were worshiping the Lord and fasting, the Holy Spirit said, "Set apart for me Barnabas and Saul for the work to which I have called them." So after they had fasted and prayed, they placed their hands on them and sent them off. (Acts 13:1–3)

What sacrifice did the church of Antioch make by commissioning these five for ministry elsewhere? _____

_____

_____

What visible return do you think the church received by sending them out? _____

_____

_____

How has your church made similar sacrifices? _____

_____

_____

God, whom I serve with my whole heart in preaching the gospel of his Son, is my witness how constantly I remember you in my prayers at all times; and I pray that now at last by God's will the way may be opened for me to come to you. I long to see you so that I may impart to you some spiritual gift to make you strong—that is, that you and I may be mutually encouraged by each other's faith. (Romans 1:9–12)

How did Paul feel toward the believers at Rome? _____

_____

_____

Why was he so anxious to visit them? _____

_____

_____

What did he hope to accomplish as a result of his visit? _____

_____

_____

MY RESPONSE

In the business realm it is not unusual to have a portfolio of investments and to keep a record of the amount invested and the amount of return. If discipleship involves investing ourselves in people, what would your spiritual portfolio look like? To find out, answer the following questions.

1. What have I invested and in whom? _____

_____

_____

2. What has been the return for the body of Christ? _____

_____

_____

3. Who has made a similar investment in me? _____

_____

_____

4. What kind of sacrifice did they make? _____

_____

_____

5. What return has there been for the body of Christ? _____

_____

_____

CONCLUSION

One of the greatest obstacles we face in making disciples is the church's tendency to allocate its resources based on the amount of return it will receive for the time, effort, and money it has expended. The church itself may not reap an immediate benefit from its discipleship effort, but the body of Christ does. The New Testament church of Antioch understood this principle and sent some of its most skilled members to make disciples elsewhere. A discipleship strategy that is based solely on the benefit the church receives in return robs God.

PRAYER

Make a list of those in whom you can invest yourself and begin praying for them. Ask God for an opportunity to make disciples.

u n i t   t w e l v e

THE
CORPORATE CONTEXT
OF DISCIPLESHIP

l e s s o n   o n e

A
GROUP
EFFORT

KEY PASSAGE: *It was he who gave some to be apostles, some to be prophets, some to be evangelists, and some to be pastors and teachers, to prepare God's people for works of service, so that the body of Christ may be built up until we all reach unity in the faith and in the knowledge of the Son of God and become mature, attaining to the whole measure of the fullness of Christ.*
(Ephesians 4:11–13)

WISE WORDS

Do walls then make Christians?

VICTORINUS

Fellowship with God inevitably brings fellowship with other Christians within the body of the church. The apostle John indicates this in the opening verses of his first letter: "That which we have seen and heard we proclaim also to you, so that you may have fellowship with us; and our fellowship is with the Father and with his Son Jesus Christ" (1 Jn. 1:3). Here are two fellowships: with God and with other Christians. Yet nothing in this verse indicates that either one of them can be had without the other.

JAMES MONTGOMERY BOICE

THOUGHT STARTER

What are some things that can only be done in a group? _____

_____

_____

Why is the group so important? _____

_____

_____

What reasons do some Christians give when they stop attending church? _____

_____

_____

Do you think these are valid? Why or why not? _____

_____

_____

SCRIPTURE STUDY

In his autobiography, Augustine told the story of the Roman orator and educator Victorinus. He was a noted philosopher and a tutor to many of the members of the Roman senate. A statue had been erected in his honor in the Roman forum. He was deeply interested in pagan philosophy but had also studied Christian literature. In fact, at one point he even told Simplicianus, the bishop of Milan, "I want you to understand that I am already a Christian." Without hesitating, the bishop shot back, "I will not believe it, nor will I rank you among Christians, unless I see you in the Church of Christ." Victorinus laughed and replied, "Do walls then make Christians?"

Victorinus had grasped an important biblical truth. Walls do not make a Christian. The church is not a building. It is made up of people who have been joined to Christ by faith. But his smug reply suggested that he had missed the real significance of the Bible's teaching on the nature of the church. Spiritual growth in the Christian life is not a purely individual matter. There is a corporate dimension to the life of discipleship.

Read Ephesians 4:11–16. Then answer the following questions.

What provision has God made to insure that believers grow from spiritual infancy to full maturity? _____

_____

_____

In what sense, according to this passage, is discipleship a group effort? _____

_____

_____

Does this make the individual less or more responsible for his or her spiritual growth? Explain. _____

_____

_____

Read Hebrews 10:19–25. Then answer the following questions.

What three things does the writer of Hebrews tell his readers to do in view of the assurance of the confidence they have with Christ as their High Priest?

1. _____

_____

2. _____

_____

3. _____

_____

The writer of Hebrews mentions several things that contribute to healthy congregational life. What are they?

_____

_____

_____

What must be done if we are to "spur one another on toward love and good deeds"? _____

_____

_____

Does this corporate dimension to our spiritual life become less important or more important over time? _____

_____

_____

Why do you think some of these Hebrew Christians had given up meeting together (cf. Hebrews 10:23–34)?

_____

_____

_____

The fact that believers have been given direct access to God through Christ does not remove the need for a corporate dimension to one's spiritual life. The confidence we have with Christ as our High Priest is one of the things that should prompt us to carefully consider how we can motivate one another to love and good deeds. This, in turn, underscores the need to be in community. The disciple's spiritual growth occurs best when it takes place in an environment where it can be nurtured by the encouragement of others.

Consequently, you are no longer foreigners and aliens, but fellow citizens with God's people and members of God's household, built on the foundation of the apostles and prophets, with Christ Jesus himself as the chief cornerstone. In him the whole building is joined together and rises to become a holy temple in the Lord. And in him you too are being built together to become a dwelling in which God lives by his Spirit. (Ephesians 2:19–22)

Therefore, rid yourselves of all malice and all deceit, hypocrisy, envy, and slander of every kind. Like newborn babies, crave pure spiritual milk, so that by it you may grow up in your salvation, now that you have tasted that the Lord is good. As you come to him, the living Stone—rejected by men but chosen by God and precious to him—you also, like living stones, are being built into a spiritual house to be a holy priesthood. (1 Peter 2:1–5)

What similarities do you see between Paul's description of the church in Ephesians 2:19–22 and Peter's description in 1 Peter 2:1–5? _____

_____

_____

In what ways do these descriptions indicate that the believer's spiritual life is a group effort? _____

_____

_____

MY RESPONSE

1. How would you respond to a friend who said, "I read my Bible regularly and pray. I am living for God on a daily basis. I also share my faith. Why do I need to attend church?" _____

_____

_____

2. How would you rate your satisfaction with your own commitment to congregational life?

Not Committed   **Very Committed**

1   2   3   4   5

What room for improvement do you see? _____

_____

_____

What do you need to do to better obey the command of Hebrews 10:19–25? _____

_____

_____

CONCLUSION

It is true that walls do not make a Christian. Buildings are not essential to the Christian life, but the church is. The Christian life is a life in community with other believers. This is especially important when it comes to discipleship. Discipleship is often regarded as a "private" exercise. It is seen as a matter of one's individual practice of Bible study, prayer, and personal obedience. The biblical context of discipleship, however, is corporate in nature. If discipleship is a "people" thing, it is equally true that it is also a "group" thing. God works through the church to promote the believer's spiritual health.

PRAYER

Pray for your church, its leaders, and its ministries. Ask God to use it in your life to spur you on to love and good works.

l e s s o n   t w o

A
COMMON
GOAL

KEY PASSAGE: *Finally, brothers, good-by. Aim for perfection, listen to my appeal, be of one mind, live in peace. And the God of love and peace will be with you.*
(2 Corinthians 13:11)

WISE WORDS

On the Lord's day assemble and break bread and give thanks, having first confessed your sins, that your sacrifice may be pure. If any have a dispute with his fellow, let him not come to the assembly till they be reconciled, that your sacrifice be not polluted.

THE DIDACHE (SECOND CENTURY A.D.)

I believe in . . . the Holy Church.

THE APOSTLES CREED (C. 340 A.D.)

THOUGHT STARTER

What should the purpose of the church be? _____

_____

_____

How is this reflected in your own church's services and ministries? _____

_____

_____

If all churches have the same purpose, should all churches be alike? Why or why not? _____

_____

_____

SCRIPTURE STUDY

Discipleship is the process of edifying the church for the purpose of maturity. This is a collective effort with a collective result. Consequently, it takes a multitude of people to accomplish this goal. Although the methods may vary, the end result should be the same for every church: spiritual maturity. In this respect, every church has the same mission. However, they do not all carry out that mission in the same way.

Then Jesus came to them and said, "All authority in heaven and on earth has been given to me. Therefore go and make disciples of all nations, baptizing them in the name of the Father and of the Son and of the Holy Spirit, and teaching them to obey everything I have commanded you. And surely I am with you always, to the very end of the age."
(Matthew 28:18–20)

Again Jesus said, "Peace be with you! As the Father has sent me, I am sending you." (John 20:21)

What does Jesus say is the church's primary mission? _____

_____

_____

Does He describe the methodology that the church should use in carrying out the mission? _____

_____

_____

What does He say about the manner in which the church is to carry out its mission? _____

_____

_____

The church's mission of making disciples has been clearly defined by Christ. Although Jesus speaks of the church's methods in sweeping terms—baptizing and teaching—he does not spell out its methodology in detail. This means individual congregations that are all working toward the same goal of making disciples may look radically different from one another as they carry out their mission.

MY RESPONSE
1. If you were to ask the average member of your church to define its mission, what kind of answer do you think you would receive? _____

_____

_____

2. Do you think you would get a different answer if you were to ask this same question of the pastor? _____

_____

_____

3. How might an awareness of your church's mission change the way you worship on Sunday? _____

_____

_____

4. How might such an awareness change what you do during the week? _____

_____

_____

CONCLUSION

God has an agenda for the church. He has given the church a mission that is people-focused and Christ-centered. It is the task of proclaiming the gospel of Christ and helping those who respond to the gospel to grow up in Christ. This is true of every congregation in every place. It does not change with time, culture, or congregational size. People maturing in Christ, then, should be the ultimate measure of success for any church. Every individual believer and every congregation ought to ask two fundamental questions. First, "Are we doing what Christ has called us to do?" Second, "Do we increasingly reflect Christ in our services, ministries, and actions?" No matter where it meets or what its size, the church's goal is the same. It is to make disciples and use its ministries to help others attain "to the whole measure of the fullness of Christ."

PRAYER

Write a personal mission statement that expresses how you feel about your place within the broader scope of the church's mission. When you are satisfied with it, read it aloud and pray a prayer of commitment.

_____

_____

_____

_____

_____

_____

THE
BODY OF
CHRIST

KEY PASSAGE: *Just as each of us has one body with many members, and these members do not all have the same function, so in Christ we who are many form one body, and each member belongs to all the others.* (Romans 12:4–5)

WISE WORDS

Alone I cannot serve the Lord effectively, and he will spare no pains to teach me this. He will bring things to an end, allowing doors to close and leaving me ineffectively knocking my head against a wall until I realize that I need the help of the Body as well as of the Lord.

WATCHMAN NEE

Church-goers are like coals in a fire. When they cling together, they keep the flame aglow; when they separate, they die out.

BILLY GRAHAM

THOUGHT STARTER

If you had to lose one of the members of your body but could choose which one it would be, which member would you select? _____

_____

_____

Why do you think the Scriptures compare the church to the human body? _____

_____

_____

SCRIPTURE STUDY

The idea of community is not unique to the New Testament. It was an important theme in the Old Testament as well. The Law of Moses often called God's people to gather as a congregation for worship.

What role does community play in the following passages?

Exodus 12:16 _____

_____

Numbers 8:9–10 _____

_____

Deuteronomy 4:10 _____

_____

How is the nation of Israel described in the passages below?

Leviticus 4:14 _____

_____

Leviticus 24:14 _____

_____

Joshua 22:15–16 _____

_____

1 Chronicles 28:8–9 _____

_____

What is implied by the fact that God's people are called the assembly "of the Lord"? _____

_____

_____

Although I hope to come to you soon, I am writing you these instructions so that, if I am delayed, you will know how people ought to conduct themselves in God's household, which is the church of the living God, the pillar and foundation of the truth. (1 Timothy 3:14–15)

How is Paul's description of the church as "the church of the living God" similar to the descriptions of God's people in the verses above? _____

_____

_____

When Paul is saying that the church is "God's household," what is he implying about the church? _____

_____

_____

Now you are the body of Christ, and each one of you is a part of it. (1 Corinthians 12:27)

How does Paul describe the church in this verse? _____

_____

_____

What does it imply about the believer's relationship to Jesus Christ? _____

_____

_____

What does it imply about the believer's relationship to other believers? _____

_____

_____

When the Scriptures speak of the church as the body of Christ, they point to two important dimensions of its relationship. The first is the church's relationship to Christ. Those who are in Christ have been joined to Christ by faith. Jesus is both the church's builder and the foundation upon which it is built (Matthew 16:18; 1 Corinthians 3:11). However, the analogy of the body also points to the fact that believers who have been joined to Christ have also been joined to one another.

The body is a unit, though it is made up of many parts; and though all its parts are many, they form one body. So it is with Christ. For we were all baptized by one Spirit into one body—whether Jews or Greeks, slave or free—and we were all given the one Spirit to drink. Now the body is not made up of one part but of many. If the foot should say, "Because I am not a hand, I do not belong to the body," it would not for that reason cease to be part of the body. And if the ear should say, "Because I am not an eye, I do not belong to the body," it would not for that reason cease to be part of the body. If the whole body were an eye, where would the sense of hearing be? If the whole body were an ear, where would the sense of smell be? But in fact God has arranged the parts in the body, every one of them, just as he wanted them to be. If they were all one part, where would the body be? (1 Corinthians 12:12–19)

Who is it that makes the body of Christ "one unit"? _____

_____

_____

What, according to these verses, does every member of the body of Christ have in common? _____

_____

_____

How do they differ from one another? _____

_____

_____

Why might the members Paul mentions be tempted to say, "I am not part of the body"? _____

_____

_____

What makes this unthinkable? _____

_____

_____

We may feel that our contribution to the body of Christ is so insignificant that the church can function without us. Just as the human body cannot function on the basis of one organ alone, the body of Christ needs all its members. Every believer contributes to the overall health of the church. Our gifts and abilities may not be as glamorous as those possessed by others, but they are vitally needed.

Read 1 Corinthians 12:20–27. Then answer the following questions.

How is the attitude described in these verses the opposite of that described in 1 Corinthians 12:12–19? _____

_____

_____

Why do you think some believers might feel this way? _____

_____

_____

How does Paul correct this faulty thinking? _____

_____

_____

What does he say about those members of the body that seem to be insignificant? _____

_____

_____

The Christian life is not a beauty contest in which those who have spectacular gifts are more pleasing to God than those who exercise the more mundane gifts. In fact, those members of the body who seem to be weaker are actually indispensable. The church's weaker or unimpressive members are essential to its health.

MY RESPONSE

1. *If you were to use a part of the human body to describe your place in the body of Christ, which member would you choose?* _____

_____

_____

2. *How has your view of yourself changed as a result of this study?* _____

_____

_____

3. *Write the name of someone you know who might be described as a "weaker" or "less honorable" member of the body of Christ.* _____

_____

_____

4. How can you express your appreciation to that person for their presence in the body of Christ? _____

_____

_____

CONCLUSION

The practical result of being joined to one another in Christ is that we need other believers to grow spiritually. There is an equally important corollary to this truth. If we need other believers, then other believers also need us. There is a mutual dependency between the various members of the body of Christ. It is possible to overlook either of these truths in our approach to the Christian life. We may think that we are unimportant or we may view others as insignificant. Every member contributes to the overall well-being of the church. There are no unnecessary members.

PRAYER

Write the names of at least one person in your church whose spiritual gift has made them prominent and of someone who has one of the "lesser" gifts. Thank God for each and pray for their ministry. Pray that God will help you to realize your full potential in serving Him and to maintain a proper attitude toward yourself and others.

A COMMUNITY OF ENCOURAGEMENT

KEY PASSAGE: *See to it, brothers, that none of you has a sinful, unbelieving heart that turns away from the living God. But encourage one another daily, as long as it is called Today, so that none of you may be hardened by sin's deceitfulness.*
(Hebrews 3:12–13)

WISE WORDS

Correction does much, but encouragement does more. Encouragement after censure is as the sun after a shower.
JOHANN WOLFGANG VON GOETHE

Encouragement is oxygen to the soul.
GEORGE M. ADAMS

THOUGHT STARTER

Think of a time when someone encouraged you. How did the person go about it? _____

_____

_____

What made this so encouraging to you? _____

_____

_____

Think of a time when someone discouraged you. How did it differ from the incident you described above? _____

_____

_____

How does this help you to understand the nature of encouragement? _____

_____

_____

SCRIPTURE STUDY

We often act as if the ability to encourage others should come naturally. Perhaps this is why we sometimes find it lacking in the church. In reality, we must make a careful study of others in order to encourage them effectively. The writer of Hebrews told his readers to "consider" how to spur one another on to love and good deeds (Hebrews 10:24). This Greek term meant to "contemplate" or "look closely" at something. It is a command to make a careful study of others for the specific purpose of spurring them on to love and action.

Read the passages listed below. Use the chart to list why the encouragement was needed, the kind of encouragement needed, and how the encouragement was expressed.

	Why was it needed?	What kind was needed?	How did it take place?
Deuteronomy 3:21–28			
Judges 7:9–15			
Acts 11:19–23			
Acts 14:19–23			
Acts 15:22–34			
Romans 15:1–7			
2 Corinthians 7:4–13			

MY RESPONSE

1. Who do you know who needs to be encouraged? What kind of circumstances have created this need? _____

_____

_____

2. What sort of encouragement is most needed at this time? _____

_____

_____

3. How can God use you to provide encouragement to that person? _____

_____

_____

4. What do you need to do in order to follow through? _____

_____

_____

CONCLUSION

Encouragement takes many forms. It may be expressed as a kind word and a pat on the shoulder. At other times it may take the form of a sharp kick (figuratively speaking) in the seat of the pants. It takes a careful study of the individual and the situation to know what kind of encouragement is needed and how it should be expressed. One of the greatest challenges in exercising the church's ministry of mutual encouragement is striking the right balance. If we want to be truly encouraging to others in the body of Christ, we must work at it. All this must be done with an awareness of our dependency upon the Holy Spirit who is the ultimate source of all encouragement in the body of Christ.

PRAYER

Pray for those you know who need encouragement. Ask God to use you today to encourage someone else.

A
REMEDY FOR
WORLDLINESS

KEY PASSAGE: *You are still worldly. For since there is jealousy and quarreling among you, are you not worldly? Are you not acting like mere men?*
(1 Corinthians 3:3)

WISE WORDS

I thought when I became a Christian I had nothing to do but just to lay my oars in the bottom of the boat and float along. But I soon found that I would have to go against the current.
D. L. MOODY

If society becomes corrupt like a dark night or stinking fish, there's no sense in blaming society. That's what happens when fallen human society is left to itself and human evil is unrestrained and unchecked. The question to ask is, "Where is the church?"
JOHN STOTT

THOUGHT STARTER

How would you define "worldliness"? _____

_____

_____

Do you know a Christian whom you would describe as "worldly"? If so, why would you characterize the person this way? _____

_____

_____

What is the opposite of worldliness? _____

_____

_____

SCRIPTURE STUDY

The background for the church's ministry of mutual encouragement is its obligation to be holy. The church is already holy as far as its position before God is concerned. Its members are described in Scripture as "saints," a "holy priesthood," and a "holy nation" (2 Corinthians 1:1; 8:4; 9:1; Ephesians 1:1; Philippians 1:1; 1 Peter 2:5–9). Yet we also have an obligation to live out the spiritual reality of this calling in our daily practice.

Avoid every kind of evil. (1 Thessalonians 5:22)

For the grace of God . . . teaches us to say "No" to ungodliness and worldly passions, and to live self-controlled, upright and godly lives in this present age, while we wait for the blessed hope—the glorious appearing of our great God and Savior, Jesus Christ, who gave himself for us to redeem us from all wickedness and to purify for himself a people that are his very own, eager to do what is good. (Titus 2:11–14)

These verses speak of both negative and positive dimensions to the church's obligation to be holy. What is the negative dimension? _____

_____

_____

How does Paul describe the positive alternative? _____

_____

_____

Read John 17:15–24. Then answer the following questions.

How did Jesus describe His disciples' relationship to the world? _____

_____

_____

In what way is our relationship to the world like Christ's? _____

_____

_____

What does Christ want the world to see when it looks at the church? _____

_____

_____

What will enable the church to remain unstained by the world while remaining in it? _____

_____

_____

Notice that Christ's prayer for His disciples does not ask God to make the church "otherworldly." This is already true of us. We are not of the world because Christ is not of it. It is a state rather than a practice. However, while it is impossible for the church to be "of" the world, it is possible for the church to behave in a worldly manner.

Read 1 Corinthians 3:1–7. Then answer the following questions.

How does Paul describe the Corinthian believers? _____

_____

_____

What was the nature of their "worldly" behavior? _____

_____

_____

Worldliness in the Corinthian church was not primarily a matter of dress or choice of entertainment. It was reflected in the believers' ability to respond to God's Word and their attitude toward one another. They displayed a worldly attitude when they became jealous of one another and divided into factions over their favorite Bible teachers. Worldly behavior such as jealousy and quarreling kept these believers from growing.

Read 2 Corinthians 6:14—7:1. Then answer the following questions.

In 2 Corinthians 6:14–15 the apostle asks the Corinthians a series of questions. What point is he trying to make with them? _____

_____

_____

What motivation does he give for living the kind of lifestyle described here? _____

_____

_____

According to 2 Corinthians 7:1, what is the positive alternative to a lifestyle of worldliness? _____

_____

_____

Do not love the world or anything in the world. If anyone loves the world, the love of the Father is not in him. For everything in the world—the cravings of sinful man, the lust of his eyes and the boasting of what he has and does—comes not from the Father but from the world. The world and its desires pass away, but the man who does the will of God lives forever. (1 John 2:15–17)

John identifies three symptoms of a worldly attitude in these verses. What are they?

1. _____

_____

2. _____

_____

3. _____

_____

What does he say is the problem with worldliness? _____

_____

_____

What is the alternative? _____

_____

_____

John defined worldliness as "the cravings of sinful man, the lust of his eyes and the boasting of what he has and does" (1 John 2:16). The trouble with worldliness is that it does not originate from the Father. Because it cannot last, it cannot ultimately satisfy. Even now all that is of the world is in the process of passing away.

MY RESPONSE

1. Where do you struggle most with worldliness? _____

_____

_____

2. What steps are you currently taking to guard against it? _____

_____

_____

3. What "negative" (that is, avoiding) measures do you need to take to avoid worldly attitudes and behavior?

_____

_____

_____

4. What positive measures should you take? _____

_____

_____

CONCLUSION

In the Scriptures the world is both the domain of Satan and the realm of the flesh. Whenever we behave in a "worldly" fashion, we act in a way that is contrary to Christ's interests. We are in the world, but we are not of it. Christ loves the world, but He does not love worldliness. The biblical notion of separation from the world is a positive concept. It is the result of a commitment to a personal relationship with God through faith in Jesus Christ. In 1 John 1:5 the apostle warns that the love of worldliness and love for God are mutually exclusive. This means that the ultimate remedy for worldliness is a love for God.

PRAYER

Ask God to increase your awareness of His love for you and of your love for Him as a barrier against worldliness.

True Discipleship

The Art of Following Jesus

**When a coworker or friend watches you
in operation, does he see a reflection of Christ?**

What sets Christians apart as disciples? Discipleship is
not primarily a matter of what we do it is an outgrowth of
what we are. If this is true, others should be able to see
the proof of the reality of our commitment to Christ reflected in the way we live.

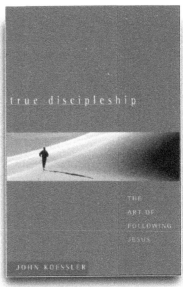

ISBN: 978-0-8024-1642-1

"Discipleship is faith expressed in real life, everyday, in
every way", says noted author and lifelong disciple John Koessler. But there is more to it
than merely watching your language on the loading dock or dropping a few coins in a
charity donation box. At its heart, discipleship is a living relationship with the Christ we love,
serve and seek to imitate. For most of us there is room in this relationship for considerable
improvement.

MOODY
Publishers

From the Word to Life

1-800-678-6928 www.MoodyPublishers.com